Idris Tawfiq holds a degree ... ...ersity of Manchester, and theology from the Pontifical University of St Thomas Aquinas in Rome. He has taught religious studies in both Britain and Egypt. Tawfiq, a Roman Catholic priest before his conversion to Islam, continues to write for many newspapers and journals around the world, including the *Middle East Times*.

Idris Tawfiq's popular lectures and broadcasts on Islam are justly celebrated. He lives in Cairo.

GARDENS *of* DELIGHT

A SIMPLE INTRODUCTION TO ISLAM

IDRIS TAWFIQ

STACEY
INTERNATIONAL

GARDENS OF DELIGHT

Published by
Stacey International
128 Kensington Church Street
London W8 4BH
Telephone: +44 (0)20 7221 7166 Fax: +44 (0)20 7792 9288
E-mail: info@stacey-international.co.uk
www.stacey-international.co.uk

ISBN: 978-1-9052995-0-8

© Idris Tawfiq 2007

The right of Idris Tawfiq to be identified as the author of this work
has been asserted by him in accordance with the Copyright, Designs
and Patents Act of 1988.

CIP Data: A catalogue record for this book is available from the British Library

Printing & Binding: Oriental Press, Dubai

Foreword

The Message that was brought to Mohammed by the angel Gabriel in the deserts of Arabia was not a new one. Rather it was a continuation of the single revelation from God to creation since the beginning of humanity; the message of all prophets aforetime: believe in God and thereafter be upright. However this message was too potent for the powers that be which surrounded Mohammed. Livelihoods, money and authority rested on continuing the pilgrimage business that had grown up around the 300-plus gods that made up the religion of the region.

Mohammed, trusted beyond all others before his prophethood was now shunned by the ruling elite. With the status quo under threat, the ruling tribes were not prepared to accept these usurpers in their midst and persecuted any who declared belief in One God. To protect his followers, Mohammed told them to flee to a righteous and just ruler, the Christian King of Abyssinia, the Negus.

Hotly pursued by tribesmen, this small band of Muslims had to quickly explain themselves and their beliefs to the Royal court. They quoted from the chapter of the Qur'an called Mary, which details the Muslim view of Jesus and his virgin mother. Drawing a line in the sand with his staff, the Negus said to the Muslims, 'The difference between you and us is as this line.'

On that line however we have built impenetrable armoured walls. We stage look out posts along its now great boundary. Instead of recognising our shared human condition we look on and see only The Other. Tales of each other's differences reach the ears of the populations of both sides of the wall, and the fear of the unknown on the other side grows and grows.

For those of us who have lived both sides of the now great wall, we know that the two worlds are as one in reality. There are differences, but these differences are there to be enjoyed, as one might enjoy different flowers in a beautiful garden. Variety of God's creation in the mind of a Muslim is a reflection of God's creative capacity, for only God is Unity. As the Qur'an says, 'We have created you into nations and tribes, so that you may know one another not so that you may hate one another.'

And yet, in a world where we have instance global

communication and access, our capacity to reach out to 'The Other' seems ever more limited. Instead of expanding our minds and hearts we have turned inward on ourselves. Paralysed by fear, we retreat down into our trenches.

But as a the companion of the Prophet, Rabat Ibn Arratt said, 'After this night of darkness there must be a dawn.' There are growing numbers of people across the world who are refusing to see each other in the two-dimensional caricature forms presented to them. Instead, there are reaching out and finding human beings, with human hearts and human lives. Silencing their fears, individuals from both sides of the great wall are realising that whilst there are differences in culture, language and belief, the beating of the human heart in the other is the same.

These brave individuals who have crossed the great mental gulfs created by fear and mistrust should be helped. Artists, musicians, sportsmen, writers and all in the public arena are surely obligated to use their great skills to be bridges. Business leaders with eyes on profits have to realise that trade is best served by global communities who communicate. Politicians who realpolitik and with only national interests at heart have to be made to realise that the real interests of their people are best served by the increase of understanding and mutual respect rather than the spreading of fear. Ultimately ordinary people living alongside each other must reach out and become neighbours, and realise that in the global village every one is a neighbour.

Some would say that such thoughts are idealistic, as if

idealism is something to be despised. However the alternatives are too frightening to contemplate. Ultimately those who promote a clash of civilisations thesis do so to the detriment of all people who simply want to work hard, raise their families and live a peaceful existence. I have never met a human being who does not want to lead a secure life, to be treated with respect and to have the chance to live in dignity. If this is what we all want, then ultimately it is up to us to achieve, and we only have ourselves to blame if we fail.

Sarah Joseph
Editor, Emel Magazine
London, May 2007

Chapter One

Setting the Scene

If you've seen Ridley Scott's film, *The Kingdom of Heaven*, you'll be as surprised as many others in the cinema to see how the Muslims are shown in quite a good light. Neither monsters nor villains, they come across as quite civilised. In fact, the only barbarians in the film are a group of Crusaders who have forgotten and forsaken their noble cause.

If you had been to see the film in any cinema in the Arab world you would have been as much taken by the reaction of the audience as anything on the screen itself. Consisting mostly of young men, you would have seen the audience sitting on the edge of their seats, spellbound as they saw for the first time on screen Islam being presented in a positive light by Hollywood. Used to being the object of fear and of blame, these young Muslim men believed that for the first time they were seeing the West portray Muslims as good. After a daily television diet of suicide bombs and terrorist attacks they could hardly believe their eyes.

Incidentally, those Muslim young men in the cinema are the same as young men the world over who go to the cinema; they have the same cares and worries as anyone else. They are there for an evening out with their friends. They, too, dream of having a good job and settling down with the girl of their dreams to one day start a family. The only difference is that after the film they will go out together for an orange juice, rather than a beer, and they won't take their girlfriends along, since that will only happen once they are engaged.

You have only to turn on a television set in any part of the Western hemisphere to be convinced that Islam is the religion of terrorism. Muslims feel that after the horrifying events of September 11, 2001 in the United States, or the subsequent bombings in Madrid or London or Sharm El-Sheikh, that there is not an explosion or a loud noise to be heard in any large city, be it the result of a leaking gas pipe or a car exhaust back-firing, and all eyes will look to Islam as its cause. The very name 'Islamic' has become associated in many people's minds with suicide bombs and suspicious characters intent on evil. Wearing the Muslim veil, far from being a symbol of modesty, has become, for many, a symbol of the oppression of women, and of religious extremism.

Where has this image come from, that makes Islam seem so violent, so aggressive, so uncompromising in its dealings with others? Daily news coverage brings to our screens images of extreme violence from Iraq and Palestine. Arabs boarding any aeroplane feel that they are looked upon with suspicious eyes not only by airport security, but by passengers, too, fearing for their own safety.

And yet when IRA violence was at its height in Northern Ireland in the 1970s and 80s, no one spoke of Roman Catholic terrorists. The Roman Catholic Church was not singled out for criticism. When the Basque separatist group, ETA, carry out attacks in Spain, no one talks about Christian terrorists. So why single out Islam?

Whilst all people of good will would unhesitatingly condemn the bombs which kill innocent men, women and children, many Muslims once again see an anomaly, a double standard. After the barbaric terrorist bombings in Madrid and London the whole of Europe observed a moment of silence to commemorate the dead, and rightly so. Yet, daily, innocent women and children are being killed in Palestine and their deaths hardly warrant a mention on the television news. Many young Muslims might then ask, are the deaths of Palestinian civilians not worth as much as the deaths of civilians in the West? The British Prime Minister, Tony Blair, was right when he said that the underlying causes of these terror attacks need to be addressed. The following pages consider these questions.

Many Muslims are, however, their own worst enemy. The image that many give to the world is a false image of Islam. Islam is not violent. The idea of a 'Muslim terrorist' is abhorrent to true Islam. The purpose of this opening chapter is to acknowledge that misunderstandings do exist, on both sides, and these misunderstandings allow falsehood to creep in. We can, of course, point to examples and to individuals who reinforce these wrong notions of Islam. Many in the Western world are terrified of Islam because of the false notions they have about it. The world's media have a lot to answer for, playing as they do upon people's fears. After all, they are looking for headlines, and violence makes a gripping story.

Let us take a step back. The West, and Western Europe in particular, has long had a fascination with the Orient. The Arab world has provoked admiration, fear and wonder. Shakespeare's Othello, the Moor of Venice, is a dark character in every sense, eaten up by jealousy, and designed to put fear into the hearts of children. Shakespeare did not choose an Indian or a Spaniard or an African as his villain, he chose an Arab Muslim. The crusades, of course, were the first real contact between east and west. Crusader knights went off to the Holy Land not only to recapture the Holy Places from the infidel but to make their fortune, to start over again in a new world of mystery. They brought back from Jerusalem and Damascus stories of Saracen brutality and torture by their heathen opponents, as well as tales of ravishing beauty and mystique. Veiled Arab women, goblets of pure gold and silver, camels, unheard of flowers and fruits, and fantastic jewels were all part of the fantasy. Forever labelled as the ones who desecrated the holy sepulchre of the saviour or who slaughtered thousands of innocent civilians, the Moors, and the Muslims, became fixed in people's minds as the villains. Story grew out of story and the imagination of the European ran wild.

When the crusades ended, the Moors were already well established in southern Spain and they would advance as far even as Vienna. For most people, though, the Muslim world became once more an unknown world, a world unvisited. All that remained in the popular imagination were memories from the past. Visitors from the Orient to the courts of Europe brought with them gifts of camels and elephants, fine silks and brocade. Ambassadors to the Sultan's court brought back tales of fabulous wealth and luxury beyond imagining, coupled with stories of slaves and concubines. Mingled with the stories of magnificence were tales of excess and cruelty, beheading and blind obedience.

The interiors of some of the Islamic palaces where *The Kingdom of Heaven*'s scenes are set are beautiful, places where beautiful things are cherished and held in honour. Indeed, the legacy of Islamic art that spread all the way across North Africa to southern Spain is exquisite. Advances in mathematics, science and calligraphy, to name a few, bequeathed to the world by Islamic scholars, are remarkable. Islamic ceramics, glassware and architecture have had a profound impact on the world's heritage.

The nineteenth-century artists and writers who travelled to the Muslim lands in search of exotic inspiration confirmed popular notions by bringing back artefacts and paintings of mosques, harems and Arab horsemen. Many places they visited, they did so clandestinely, adding to the sense of mystery. These Orientalists, often disguised as women in veils and long black clothes, sought to penetrate forbidden worlds, sometimes entering the holy city of Makkah itself. In short, the Muslim world had become a mystery. We often fear that which we do not understand.

With the advent of oil in the Gulf states in the 1960s and 1970s, wealthy Arab visitors started coming to London, Paris and New York, bringing with them strange customs and modes of dress. Waves of immigrants into Europe from North Africa, Turkey and South East Asia brought many people into contact with Islam for the first time.

And yet, Muslims are ordinary people. The vast majority do not have fabulous wealth. In fact, the opposite is true. Most of them get up in the morning, go to work and return in the evening to watch some television before going to bed. Nothing fanatical about that. A Muslim bus driver in Damascus goes to work in the same way as his non-Muslim counterpart in Washington. They both want to earn a living, to bring back enough money to support their families and send their children to school, maybe having enough left over for a family holiday.

If we had the ability, or the great gift, of being able to see things from another's point of view, of being able to walk in someone else's shoes, we would see that Islam as a religion is neither violent nor aggressive. We would see that Muslims believe Islam to be the religion of peace, and the answer to man's problems. If we can suspend our disbelief just long enough to hear what the other has to say, Islam might be given the chance to speak for itself.

So, in this opening chapter we are trying to clear away some of the obstacles which might prevent us from understanding what Islam really is. Non-Muslims cannot be introduced to Islam without us saying a few words about certain ways of behaving that seem puzzling and strange, even offensive, to those not used to them. As we will continue to repeat: misconceptions and misunderstandings breed mistrust.

We must say something at the start about the way Islam treats women. Or rather, we need to say something about what people think it says. Remember, different cultures and different backgrounds look at different things in different ways. It doesn't make them right or wrong, just different. If I look at a painting from the front I will see something totally different from someone who looks at it from the back, although we are both looking at the same object. Where we are coming from, then, influences our understanding.

Let us give an example. Muslim women in the Gulf States, Iran and Afghanistan, for example, are swathed in black from head to toe, exposing only their hands and part of their face. If not used to this, many would instantly see it as cruel, oppressive, and old-fashioned. Indeed, as contrary to the rights that have been achieved by women over the years. This mindset sees women swathed in black as wrong, somehow a symbol of the 'empire of evil' that threatens to engulf the civilised world.

Islam requires men and women to dress modestly. It is a very common sense requirement, which recognizes that men and women have feelings towards each other that can lead to immodest ways of behaving. Muslims would point to the prevalence of promiscuity and pornography in the non-Muslim world that can result from allowing natural feelings to be given free rein. In dressing modestly, they would say, and in a way that does not excite passion between the sexes, Islam offers a way for both men and women to live in a chaste way. For most Muslim women, this would mean wearing the Muslim veil in the presence of all men who are not a part of the immediate family. In other Muslim societies women cover completely when they are outside their homes. Just suspend your disbelief for one moment and try this idea: that women might want to give themselves totally to the one they love. So much so, that the only one they want even to see them is their husband. The idea, from this point of view, is quite romantic.

Coercion has no part in Islam. Examples of coercion should not be given in order to dismiss what Islam is really about.

In an age when giving up one's seat on the bus for a lady, or holding the door open for her to pass through, has become archaic in many parts of the Western world, these things still remain firmly fixed in Muslim society, just as respect and reverence for one's elders is a matter of course.

In contrast to sensational examples used by the press, which are the exception rather than the rule, a whole book could be written about the rights which Islam gives daily to women. Her marriage dowry remains completely hers and cannot be touched by her husband, giving her a financial security beyond the marriage. A wife is entitled by right to be provided for. She doesn't have to work if she doesn't want to. The rights and the respect which Islam gives to women were revolutionary when they were first introduced into the Arabian Peninsula in the seventh century. They are no less real today. Setting aside any rights, though, one has only to visit a Muslim home to see the importance the woman has in the family. She commands deep love and respect from her children and she is loved and protected by her husband. Sitting in a Muslim family home will leave no-one in any doubt about how important the female members are. Go down to any local market in Cairo and you will see the rights of women in action. The husband will be carrying two shopping bags, his son will be sitting on his shoulder and his young daughter will be holding his hand. His wife will be walking ahead of them, checking the vegetables, monarch of all she surveys. Lived reality isn't all that the newspapers would have us believe. 'Paradise,' said the Prophet Mohammed, 'lies at the feet of your mother.'

Another thing that causes many to squint their eyes at something totally strange is the Muslim attitude to drink. Alcohol causes an obvious stumbling block for some. Muslims do not drink alcohol. Why? Because it is forbidden in the Qur'an, their holy book. Alcohol, they believe, should be shunned not only because of the physical harm it can allegedly cause to the body, but because it doesn't leave you fully in control. It clouds your thoughts, affects your judgement and lowers your ability to live an upright life. A more important reason than all this, though, is that Allah forbids it. For Muslims, that should be reason enough.

Similarly, the eating of pork is forbidden. Islamic scholars and doctors cite reasons of health, especially in hot climates, but more importantly, it is forbidden because Allah forbids it in the Qur'an.

So, with some misconceptions at least mentioned, if not altogether resolved, the story of Islam is almost ready to be told. It would be a pity if these misconceptions were allowed to diminish what Islam has to say about itself.

Not too many years ago, plans were laid for the building of a grand mosque in Rome. To be made of white marble and be visible from a great distance, this mosque would be paid for with money from Saudi Arabia. Rome's immigrant population of Muslims from North Africa and the Balkan countries would be the mosque's worshippers, but its importance in Rome was that it would be set up at the centre of the Christian faith. Public demonstrations and an outcry from right-wing groups, calling for a new crusade to stop the building of the mosque, were silenced when the Pope himself declared that the mosque should be built, as a gesture of inter-faith trust and co-operation. Rome's main mosque now stands tall amidst its surroundings.

Even in Rome the mosque had become a natural part of the scenery. A beacon of Islam in the eternal city.

Islam is the world's fastest growing religion. There are now around one billion Muslims in the world. Only eighteen per cent of all Muslims are Arab. There are more Muslims living in Indonesia than in all of North Africa and the Middle East put together, and most Muslims live east of Karachi. The United States has a Muslim population of about five million. What is truly extraordinary is that the number of people wishing to embrace Islam in the western world has actually gone up since the attacks of September 11, 2001.

In these pages, Islam will tell its own story. Sometimes, to make it more readable, the story will be accompanied by visits to places in Cairo or through the eyes of particular characters. Cairo, a city teaming with people, shouts religion from every pore. Its people, predominantly Muslim, live and breathe Islam. Their story will give life and human depth to what Islam has to say. These pages attempt to explain what Islam really is and why it is growing so fast, why it appeals so directly to the human heart.

Men and women can build bridges between nations and can lay the foundations of peace by getting to understand one another more. First of all, though, we are in desperate need to understand ourselves, to know where we stand and what we believe. Islam believes that it speaks to this need in all of us. Replacing the need for power and importance, for having more rather than being better, Muslims believe that their religion calls us to see our real worth before the Almighty and to bow down in submission to Him. It rejects the shallow selfishness that leaves us empty and wanting more and it invites us, instead, to a Garden of Delights. In the following pages we will allow Muslims to take us by the hand and walk together with us in that garden.

> O Mankind ! We created you from a single soul, Male and female, And we made you into nations and tribes, That ye may know each other. Verily, the most honoured of you In the sight of Allah Is the greatest of you in piety. Allah is All-Knowing, All-Aware.
>
> (Holy Qur'an 49: 13)

Chapter Two

Allah

Sitting in the open courtyard of Cairo's mosque of Sultan Hassan, its massively thick walls towering upwards towards heaven, makes one feel very small in comparison. Life is very fragile compared to such greatness. Considered by many Egyptians as the 'fourth' pyramid, because of its sheer size and grandeur, the mosque of Sultan Hassan is a statement of that central belief of Islam, 'Allahu Akbar,' Allah is the Greatest. Seeing the mosque filled with thousands of the faithful for Friday prayers, bowing in adoration before their Creator, fills one with awe. Row upon row of barefooted worshippers prostrate on the ground before the Almighty puts the ordinary affairs of business and of life into context. 'You alone we worship. You alone we serve,' proclaims the prayer leader. The faithful respond in humble and silent submission to Allah, 'Allah.'

Islam quite literally means 'submission.' A Muslim is one who submits totally to Allah, realising that all life comes from Him and that at the end of life on earth all must submit to His final judgement, answering personally for their deeds. The very concept is alien to those who strive to be important in this world. A Muslim declares his faith by saying that there is no Allah but Allah and that Mohammed is the messenger of Allah.

We need to understand something very important right at the start. It will help us to understand that Muslims believe in one Allah, who has no partner or equal.

Imagine that you had a really bad row with your mother, during which terrible things were said and which upset her very much. At the height of the row you picked up her favourite vase, a wedding present from your father, and smashed it on the floor. You then stormed off. However, because you love your mother very much you later went back to her, hugged and kissed her, told her many times how sorry you were. She shed a mother's tears and forgave you for what you had said and done. The row was then forgotten. No hard feelings and no lingering grudges. Yet, the vase was still smashed and no amount of forgiveness could repair it. In fact, there is nothing you could ever do to repair that broken vase.

This example can illustrate for us the main difference

between Islam and the two other major world religions which believe in one Allah, Christianity and Judaism. In the story of Adam and Eve found in the Bible, Adam sins and is forever cast out of the Garden of Eden because of his sin. For Christians and Jews that is the end of the story of Adam and Eve. Mankind inherits Adam's sin, because he passes it on since there is nothing Adam can do to make up for it. He has offended Allah and no matter how sorry he is for what he has done there is absolutely nothing he can do to repair the damage. The vase remains broken. It would need a super human to repair the vase.

In the story of Adam and Eve in the Qur'an, Adam and Eve are expelled from Paradise because of their sin. But, according to Islam, that is not the end of the story. After wandering around full of guilt, they return and receive Allah's forgiveness. The vase maker Himself repairs the vase and the sin is forgotten. We learn something very important about Allah from this incident. He is forgiving. Adam appears before Him on the plain of Arafat, near Makkah, and at a hill which has become known as the Mount of Mercy, Adam is forgiven. This is not the cruel Allah of Islam so often portrayed by non-Muslims, but rather a Allah who forgives, a Allah of Mercy and Compassion. Incidentally, the Qur'an account does not lay the blame on Eve. Adam and Eve both sin. Woman is not left to carry the blame through the ages.

Because of the two different endings to the Adam and Eve story there are different consequences. Christians and Jews believe that because of Adam's sin the world is in need of a Messiah – to save them from sin and to redeem them. Christians believe that this Messiah (which means 'Anointed One' in Hebrew) was Jesus. They believe that since Jesus was Allah's son, his sacrifice of himself on the Cross made up for the sin of Adam and 'repaired the vase.' The Qur'an could not be more specific: Jesus did not die on the cross. The Jews are still waiting for a Messiah to appear on the Temple Mount in Jerusalem to save them from their enemies.

Muslims, on the other hand, feel no need for a saviour. What would he save them from? In fact, in Islam there are no priests or mediators, no go-betweens between Allah and Man. There are no chants or spells, no secret knowledge, no popes or conclaves. The individual Muslim prays directly to Allah, and it is to Allah alone that he will one day have to answer. His knowledge of Islam comes from the Qur'an and the life and example of the one to whom it was revealed. Allah's greatness is written in the heavens and on the earth. For the Muslim, Man has only to look and he will see the fingerprints of Allah all over His creation.

Muslims believe that Islam is the natural religion of Mankind and that this religion has existed since the beginning of time. In the next chapter we will see the part that Mohammed played in Allah's revelation to Mankind and how Mohammed (peace and blessings of Allah be upon him) was the last of the prophets. All the prophets revered by Christians and Jews, including Moses and Jesus, revealed something about this one Allah, and that is why they are honoured in Islam. When someone embraces

Islam he must declare his belief in both Jesus and Moses as prophets. All the prophets called Mankind away from worshipping idols or things that were not of Allah to worshipping Allah alone. It was only with Allah's final revelation to mankind in the Holy Qur'an that this religion was perfected.

Muslims believe that Adam, the first man, was also the first Muslim. Adam was the first to worship the one Allah. Nothing could be more important to Muslims than the idea that there is only one Allah, who has no partner and who has no equal. It is believed that even before the creation of Adam, Allah gathered before Him on the plain of Arafat the souls of all the people who would ever exist on the face of the earth. As they stood before Him He revealed to them that there was no Allah but He. No one ever has the excuse to say that they never heard about this one Allah, since Allah Himself told them this long ago. It will be on this same plain of Arafat, on the Day of Judgement, that all souls will one day have to answer to Allah for their deeds.

The Holy Qur'an tells how many of Allah's prophets and messengers suffered persecution because they called mankind away from idolatry to the worship of Allah alone. And in our own, modern, age Islam calls us to reject the idols that are not of Allah and to worship Him alone. We are not to set up our own little Allahs, like work or football, and worship before their shrines, but rather to look to Allah. From the beginning of Time itself, Islam has rejected idol worship.

So what, then, is this One Allah like? According to

Islam, Allah is so great, so powerful and so different from His creation that our human minds can only think in images to describe Him. Whenever we think we know what Allah is like, whenever we think we are beginning to understand Him, we can be sure that He is not like that! Words and images fail us in trying to describe the indescribable. How could mere creatures, who live on this earth for such a limited span of time, even begin to comprehend their Creator? 'Allahu Akbar: Allah is the Greatest.' This great Allah created the heavens and the earth, the sun and the moon and all the stars. He created all things which live, all things that have ever lived and all things that will exist in the future.

He knows all things, both now and what is to come. He knows the very secrets of men's hearts. Man's only response in the face of such greatness is to bow down and worship.

> He is Allah, the Creator, the Shaper out of nothing, the Fashioner. His are the most beautiful names. All that is in the heavens and in the earth gives Him glory, and He is the Mighty, the Wise.

(Holy Qur'an 9: 24)

And yet, according to Muslim belief, even though Allah is so far from us in power and majesty and knowledge, and so different to His creation, He is also very close to each person and cares for each one. Allah listens to the prayers of the faithful and, if He wills, answers those prayers. He guides the faithful through every movement and moment of their lives. At the end of each person's life he will be judged by Allah and will be punished for ever because of his bad deeds or rewarded with Paradise for the good he has done. 'Allahu Akbar: Allah is the Greatest.' The Muslim lives his life trying to please Allah and hoping that his prayers will be heard. Life itself is a test in which Man can win the prize of Paradise and its Gardens of Delight. Allah, for the Muslim, is infinitely watchful of His Creation.

But, we ask again, is this Allah of the Muslims a harsh and cruel Allah before Whom we have to bow down in adoration? One might just as well ask is the average father of a child harsh and cruel? The answer is probably, 'no,' but the average father does sometimes need to be stern with his child or even punish or reprimand him. This does not suggest a lack of love. In fact, it breaks many a father's heart to have to appear stern or harsh with his son in order to teach him what is best. This is a poor analogy, since Allah is far greater than anything we can imagine, but it does nudge us towards the truth. The ways of Allah, according to Muslims, are unfathomable and unknowable, but His dealings with Mankind which we see in the Holy Qur'an and throughout history show us how merciful and compassionate He is.

There is a phrase in Arabic which enters almost every sentence which the Muslim utters. He uses it in every situation of life: 'Inshallah.' This translates roughly as, 'If Allah wills it to be so.' You will hear a Muslim planning the day's events, 'inshallah,' – if Allah wills it to be so. 'I will go to the shops, inshallah,' or, 'I will see you tomorrow, inshallah.' You might ask if this bus goes to town, inshallah, or describe the ingredients that go into a cake, inshallah. No-one would presume to know the future, not even five minutes into the future. That would be attempting to take away from Allah's power, and Allah has no equal. Every detail of life, from the momentous to the seemingly insignificant, is a part of Allah's plan. Nothing can ever happen that Allah does not allow to happen. His wisdom and His care encompass all things. There is nothing that He does not see or know.

Some non-Muslims, who do not understand just how deeply rooted in Islam is the notion that Allah is Great and all-knowing, may find this idea of 'inshallah' at least strange. Some may even find it amusing to suggest that fixed events, like the rising of the sun the next day, should be described 'inshallah'. Others have been heard to mimic the phrase as though it means, 'hopefully,' or 'maybe even not at all!' However, for the devout Muslim, all aspects of life are covered by Allah's care. Since Allah is the All-Knowing and the One from whom all life comes and to Whom all life will return, it is simply, for such a Muslim, a matter of fact that Allah is in control of everything. The night will only follow the day if Allah wills the night to follow day. The sun will come up tomorrow if Allah wills it to be so. Many would suggest that it is greatly reassuring that in a world beset by doubt all events, far from being coincidental or haphazard, are indeed part of a vast plan. All of our lives are lived according to Allah's plan. Nothing can happen to us that is not part of Allah's plan for the world and we can do nothing to avoid what is planned.

Even the manner and time of our death has already been determined. We are asked to co-operate in this divine plan and, in doing so, to find our happiness.

When asked, 'How are you?' a Muslim will reply, 'Ilhamdulillah,' thanks be to Allah, whether he is well or ill. In all things, he will render thanks to Allah. Another phrase, equally important for the Muslim, is 'Bismillah Ar-Rahman Ar-Rahim.' Found in the Holy Qur'an, this translates as, 'In the name of Allah, the Merciful, the Compassionate.' No action should take place without this invocation being made. No Muslim would enter a room, get on a bus, begin his work, take a sip of water without declaring it to be done in the name of Allah. All things are done in Allah's name. In a sense, all things are made holy and find their success by asking Allah to bless them. The phrase also tells us what Muslims believe Allah is like. He is not described as cruel or vengeful, but as merciful and compassionate. What a delightful description! The Creator of the heavens and the earth is actually described as the One who shows mercy and compassion.

How different this is from the descriptions of Islam you see daily on the television screens or read in the newspapers in London or New York. There you would see Islam as cruel, the religion of extremists or of terrorists. This television Islam is concerned with fighting and violence, with weapons of mass destruction. Its supposed adherents are rigid in their beliefs and unrelenting in punishing those who offend them. The bearded figures in strange clothes who we see on our television screens, often carrying weapons, are particularly frightening to Western sensibilities, conjuring up images of suicide attacks and guerilla warfare.

Yet any Muslim would tell you that Islam is the religion of peace and tolerance. The words they would use to describe it would be gentle, peaceful and beautiful, and they are bewildered and hurt and cannot understand how anyone could think otherwise. Allah is Merciful and Compassionate, they say. How could His religion be cruel?

Islam teaches that since the beginning of time, Allah has revealed Himself to Mankind, bestowing His blessings and His mercy. He has shown Himself to be oft-forgiving and abounding in compassion. Allah's will, says Islam, is that all find peace and security in Him.

But Islam poses a challenge. It is a simple fact of the human condition that Man longs for happiness. In any community, in any family, on any street we see people who want to find fulfilment in their lives. Men and women look for that perfect partner who they will spend the rest of their lives with, and with whom they will raise a family and see their children grow up and find success. Others look for satisfaction in their work, hoping that job satisfaction will be accompanied by a financial reward that helps to make life comfortable. Still others seek to find happiness in sport or music or travel. And others try to answer their need for happiness in less wholesome pursuits: drugs, sex, crime. And yet there still remains a longing in the human heart that no amount of material possessions or even loving relationships can answer. How many of us, having managed to save up for that new car, soon enough want a better one? How many, having saved for so many years to pay the deposit for an apartment or house, are soon looking for a brighter apartment or a bigger home? The clothes we have in our wardrobe never seem to be enough. The holidays we take are never long enough or exotic enough to provide rest for our weary bodies.

Why is it that the television is always switched on, even when guests visit us? Turning on the radio is one of the first things we do when getting out of bed in the morning. All of this as if silence would remind us of our loneliness, our longing. We need noise to stop us from thinking. Our restless hearts, clamouring for peace, shut out the serenity with noise.

Islam speaks right to the heart of this condition and says that there is an answer. What people are really searching for, although they don't realise it, is Allah Himself. Islam enables Man to listen to Allah Himself and respond to Him.

Let us take an analogy from Ancient Rome. The Romans were great builders and they were the masters of a great empire. An intricate network of roads made communication throughout the empire possible. At the centre of the road network was the city of Rome itself. We have taken this fact and made it a part of the English language: 'all roads lead to Rome.' And indeed they did. It was possible to travel directly to Rome from the furthest, far-flung corners of the empire on roads that were straight and well-paved. Islam tells today's world not that all roads now lead to Rome – the greatness of Rome has long since vanished – instead, we are helped to see that all roads lead to Allah. It is possible, in all the circumstances of life, to find paths that lead us to Allah. By responding to His call and listening to His promptings we can find our way out of the noise and the chaos that modern life confronts us with and we can find the peace and the calm which Islam offers, soothing our hearts and refreshing our bodies.

For Muslims, the simple Arabic phrase, La Illaha Illallah, there is no Allah but Allah, is the key which bursts open the door to life's meaning. All roads lead to Allah, the One Allah who is without partner or equal. Muslims believe that Allah has revealed Himself to Mankind in the Qur'an and has shown men and women how to know, love and serve Him in this world and given hope of happiness forever in the world to come.

The problem is that our human hearts are very stubborn and we both rebel and resist. We rebel against people telling us what to do or how to behave. We resist anyone interfering in our privacy. Islam invites us to submit, to cast aside our own logic, our own self-interest, our own plans and schemes for how things should be done. Instead, we are invited to bow in submission to something infinitely greater than ourselves, to someone Who will guide along the right path every step that we take. It may seem strange to us, at first, not to be in control, but there comes a security in knowing that the One who guides us is truly in control of all things.

The five central beliefs of Islam, on which the whole

religion is based, are called five pillars. It is as though these pillars hold up the faith of Muslims, just as pillars stop a building from falling down. The pillars, in turn, help Muslims to be faithful to what they believe. The first of these pillars we have begun to look at in this first chapter. It is called, in Arabic, 'Shahadah,' or bearing witness that there is no Allah but Allah and Mohammed is the messenger of Allah. This Shahadah is so important that it is called from the top of every minaret in the world five times a day to call the Faithful to prayer. It is the first thing that a Muslim man will whisper into the ear of his newborn baby. It is the only formula necessary for a person to declare in order to become Muslim. It is what all Muslims would hope to utter before they die. In this first chapter we have tried to talk about Allah. In the next we shall talk about Mohammed, and in the subsequent chapters we will talk about the other four pillars of Islam.

The second pillar follows on quite naturally from the first: prayer. Muslims are required to pray five times a day. Prayer is Man's response to his belief in this One Allah. The third pillar of Islam is called Zakah: giving a certain amount of one's possessions to the poor in acknowledgement that all worldly possessions come from Allah and that those who are fortunate to have possessions in this world hold them in trust from Him. The fourth pillar, which Muslims believe was revealed by Allah in the Holy Qur'an, is fasting during the month of Ramadan. The fifth and final pillar of Islam, Hajj, is the requirement of every Muslim who is able to do so to make a special pilgrimage once in his life to Makkah.

So we have started our introduction to Islam by saying that the central, most important, belief of Muslims is very simple: there is one Allah. In bending one's will to accept this idea that one Allah exists and controls the world we are then at least open to the possibility of hearing more. Islam, the religion of submission to Allah, invites us to submit totally to His will, to accept His greatness and our smallness and to prostrate ourselves on the ground before Him. When a man's forehead is touching the dust of the earth, bowing in total submission before His Creator, he is at his most vulnerable. Islam teaches that the wisdom of this world is reduced to nothing compared to the greatness of Allah. Neither the strongest man in the world nor the richest has any power or influence over his destiny. The Muslim accepts his destiny from Allah and finds his happiness in it, knowing that this destiny can lead him to Paradise.

* * *

Returning to the mosque of Sultan Hassan, the whole complex is monumental in scale. Built between 1356 and 1363, the mosque's construction almost bankrupted the state, so vast was the project. Everything about the mosque shouts greatness. We enter through a massive stone portal, dripping with stalactites carved in limestone. We wander through a cavernous and dark passageway, with walls several metres thick, before coming out into the central courtyard where our chapter began. In the centre is an enormous covered fountain for the faithful to wash before prayer. On three of the four sides are vast covered spaces where students of Islamic law would have sat at the feet of their teachers. On the fourth side is the marble and gold mihrab, pointing out the directio the sky. In the cool of the morning or in the glare of the afternoon sun, one can sit quietly pondering the vastness of Allah.

Chapter Three

Mohammed –
A Mercy to Mankind

You can't make someone love you. There is no formula or set plan of action that can inspire love from someone else. Many hearts would be satisfied if that were indeed possible! Prophet Mohammed, may Allah's peace and blessings be upon him, has a special place of honour in the heart of every Muslim. He is not just admired or respected or looked up to. He is loved. A real love that comes from the heart. Prophet Mohammed is loved by Muslims.

* * *

There is in the heart of Cairo a district whose very name inspires instant affection in the heart of every Egyptian. A district of ramshackle buildings standing alongside magnificent mosques and the ruins of palaces, the oldest university in the world, the shrine of a grandson of the Prophet and a bazaar famous throughout the Middle East. In this district you will find scantily-clad tourists jostling alongside matronly Egyptian ladies and visitors from the Gulf States, swathed in black, street hawkers and shoeshine boys in from the countryside, streetwise youths with a fast line in selling. All of life is here. The district: Al-Hussein.

Moulid An-Nabi, the birthday of the Prophet, is not a religious feast, as such. It is more a popular outbreak of joy in celebrating the birthday of someone who is loved so much. Celebrated as a national, public holiday in Egypt and many other Arab and Muslim nations, nowhere can you find this festival more celebrated than in Hussein. Packed on any ordinary weekend evening, thousands of people flock into the district for the festival. The usual tourist cafes and restaurants selling chicken and kebab are now swelled by stalls set up for a more local audience to sell pop-corn, candy-floss, toffee-apples – anything a small child could ever want his father to buy him. Toys, balloons, little drums. Street singers singing the praises of the Prophet. A scene full of fun. A celebration of the joy of Islam.

* * *

Islam has no revered founder who set up the religion. We have already said that Muslims believe that Islam has existed since the beginning of time and that the first man, Adam, was also the first Muslim. Men and women are born good by nature. There is no fault in Allah's creation.

We have indeed created man in the best of moulds.
(Holy Qur'an 95: 4)

Free from all other influences, men and women would naturally believe in One Allah, unless they were taught something different. The prophet Ibrahim (father Abraham to Christians and Jews) was a prophet of Islam, as were David and Solomon. Even the one hailed by Christians as John the Baptist, Yahya, is said to be a prophet of Islam. Moses and Jesus, too, all prophets of Islam. All of these preaching worship of One Allah and the rejection of idols. Muslims believe that the message about the One Allah revealed to Moses and Jesus became distorted and misrepresented over time. The Jews went astray, becoming preoccupied with their land and inventing laws and regulations which became a burden for men's backs. The Christians, out of an exaggerated love for Jesus, lost the spirit of what was revealed to them and began to see Jesus as divine, Allah's son who came down to earth to save mankind from sin.

Muslims believe that the Holy Qur'an is quite literally the word of Allah. They will often say, 'As Allah said in the Qur'an…' to justify an argument. Speaking of his Prophet Mohammed, Allah says (according to Muslims) in the

Qur'an, 'We have sent you but as a mercy for all mankind.' Neither a king nor a Allah, Mohammed is often referred to by Muslims quite simply as 'the best of men.' For reasons known to Allah alone, he chose a simple man of humble origin, living in the relative obscurity of the Arabian Peninsula, to bear His message, His mercy to all mankind.

An honest and noble man, loved by all who knew him even before the Revelation of Allah, Mohammed was to become the perfect example of how Islam is to be lived. His every action, thought and word would mirror the Revelation he had received. His life and example, rooted in Allah's revelation of Himself, are now the inspiration for millions of Muslims.

In Islam there are no theological formulas that need to be explained to the uninitiated by professional religious people. There are no abstruse or obscure doctrines that must be interpreted before the faithful can understand them. If there is ever a dispute over some way of living one's life, the Muslim will simply look at what Mohammed would have done or what he would have said about that situation. In the holy Qur'an and in the life and teaching of the Prophet Mohammed (may Allah's peace and blessings be upon him) the Muslim has true and sure guidance. Allah has spoken about Himself and has told Man how to live. Mohammed has responded to that Revelation.

Makkah at the time of Mohammed's birth was a centre of importance, being on the caravan routes between Yemen in the south and Syria in the north. Many traders would pass through the town on their way to do business, stopping off on the way for additional deals and for rest. Makkah also had an additional importance. It was home to the Ka'aba, the house of Allah rebuilt by Ibrahim many centuries before, and had become a centre of pilgrimage.

Thousands would flock to honour the many idols housed within the Ka'aba, offering gifts and in turn bringing added wealth to the town. The Ka'aba was also a place of sanctuary. Anyone taking refuge within its walls could claim sanctuary and would be safe from any enemies until a dispute could be resolved. All of these factors made Makkah a centre of some importance in the area.

It was so important, in fact, that many envied its position. Fifty days before the birth of Mohammed one such person, Abraha the ruler of Yemen, vowed to destroy the Ka'aba and remove the centre of pilgrimage, with all its associated trade and prestige, to Sana'a in Yemen. He approached Makkah with an army, at the head of which rode Abraha himself and an elephant. As they approached the Ka'aba the elephant sat down and refused to budge. No amount of beatings could get it to move. At the same time a flock of birds appeared, as if from nowhere, carrying large rocks, which they hurled down on Abraha's army, destroying the invading army, almost to a man. What had seemed like impending disaster for the people of Makkah had turned into a miraculous victory. Makkah and the Ka'aba were untouched.

In later years many would point to this and similar

strange events which surrounded the birth and childhood of Allah's Messenger, as wholly fitting since this was not just the birth of one man, but also the birth of a nation. They would also point to references in the Jewish Torah and the Christian Gospel promising that someone would come in the future.

We need not write here every detail of Mohammed's life, since this is covered in many other places, but a few facts will help us to understand more. His family belonged to the noble tribe of the Quraysh, which traced itself back to Ibrahim's eldest son, Ismail, and was held in high regard in Makkah and the surrounding territories. His grandfather, Abdel Muttalib, was a leading figure in Makkah, well-respected and honoured by his friends and colleagues. Mohammed was never to know his father, Abdullah, since he died just before the boy was born. Instead, he was brought up by his mother until the age of six when she, too, died and was taken from him. The young boy was placed in the care of his grandfather, but his grandfather, too, died only two years later and the young boy went to live with his uncle, Abu Talib, who was to play such a strong role in protecting and caring for the boy, even into manhood.

Before continuing with the story of Mohammed, let us pause and reflect on how Allah chooses rather strangely, according to our human wisdom. Whilst Mohammed was born of a good family, a decent family honoured by its neighbours, he was neither born to power nor wealth. Orphaned by the age of six, he lived with his uncle, not in the centre of some great and powerful city with an influence extending far beyond its boundaries, but rather in a region strategically unimportant to the world powers of the time. To modern, Western eyes, Mohammed was an orphan living in the middle of nowhere. And yet Allah took this orphaned boy, according to Islam, and made him a warner, a witness and a bearer of glad tidings to all mankind. He used His chosen instrument, who could neither read nor write, as a mercy to the nations.

Many are the stories connected with Mohammed's childhood which show that the boy was somehow special. Hindsight has a habit of always putting a rosy glow on ordinary events that took place long ago. Wishful thinking sometimes permits us to elaborate simple stories. However, many people testify to the special way in which the young Mohammed was honoured. When he was eight years old a group of people was visiting Makkah during a time of severe drought. How they longed for something to drink. No water had been seen for a long time, not even a cloud. They asked the boy's grandfather to take him with them to pray for rain. No sooner had they arrived at the Ka'aba with the child than clouds began to appear across the sky, followed by plentiful rain in abundance.

At the age of twelve he accompanied his uncle, Abu Talib, on a business trip to Syria, but on the way there they met a Christian monk who was so impressed by the boy that he insisted on entertaining them lavishly. 'This is the messenger of Allah to mankind,' the monk told them. He urged Abu Talib not to take the boy any further with him, but to send him back home for fear of enemies who might harm him.

Mohammed was sent back to Makkah.

Mohammed grew into a fine young man. He inspired love from his friends and respect from those he worked with. Working at first as a shepherd, like many prophets before him, and later on entrusted with business dealings by friends and relations, Mohammed was a good and religious man. He earned the name, Al-Amin, the trustworthy one, from those who knew him. When Mohammed was thirty-five a severe flood almost demolished the Ka'aba, causing severe damage to its foundations. The tribes of Makkah naturally wanted to rebuild it and they set about their work vigorously, replacing one stone after another. There is in the corner of the Ka'aba a special rock, set into the wall, known as the Black Stone. The Makkahns believed this Black Stone to have been brought down to earth from heaven by angels. Whichever tribe put the Black Stone back into its place would indeed be highly honoured. Indeed, they thought, only the most honourable tribe of all was worthy to do this. Therein lay the problem. None of them could agree which tribe should have the honour of replacing the Black Stone. It threatened to cause a major dispute until someone suggested that they wait for the next person to come through one of the gates to enter the precincts of the Ka'aba. They would let that person decide. What a relief it was to everyone when the first person to come through the gate was Mohammed. 'It is Al-Amin,' they said, 'the trustworthy one.' Mohammed showed great wisdom in settling the dispute. He placed a cloak on the ground, put the revered Black Stone in its centre, and then asked the tribes to each take a corner and lift the cloak. Mohammed himself then edged the Black Stone into its place. Everyone was satisfied and Mohammed's standing grew even more as a trustworthy, wise and honest man.

A deeply spiritual man, Mohammed would often go off on his own for days and nights to the cave of Hira, near Makkah, to spend time fasting and thinking about Allah. It was on one such night towards the end of the month of Ramadan that something was to happen that would change the course of human history. Allah was to reveal Himself to Mankind.

Chapter Four

Mohammed – Messenger of Allah

If you've ever watched a class of six-year-old children you'll know that, when excited, their chattering and laughing and shouting combine to produce a noise level unimaginable to man. Experienced teachers have a solution. Just at the height of the chaos the class teacher, without a sound, raises her hand and the result is electric. As if by magic, the noise stops and the little ones raise their own hands, too, until all are silently looking at the teacher, waiting for her to speak.

Muslims, too, have a similar magic. In the middle of a street brawl or a heated discussion it only takes some bystander to say, 'Salih An-Nabi,' Pray for the Prophet, and the protagonists back off, replying, 'Peace and blessings of

Allah be upon him.' How could Muslims fight when their beloved Prophet's name is invoked? Whenever Mohammed's name is spoken or written, those hearing it will say the same words, 'Peace and blessings of Allah be upon him.' In fact, in most Arab countries there is a special key on the typewriter or keyboard which, when pressed, writes 'Peace and blessings of Allah be upon him.'

* * *

So we now take up the story once more, at the point where heaven and earth were waiting with baited breath for what would happen. Mohammed, now at the age of forty, was alone in the cave, Hira, reflecting and praying, when he heard an angelic voice. The voice was that of angel Jibril (Gabriel) and it said, 'Read!' Mohammed said, 'I cannot read.' Then the angel took hold of Mohammed and squeezed him until he could almost no longer bear it. The angel again said, 'Read!' and Mohammed again replied that he could not read. The angel squeezed him again and then for a third time said:

> Read, in the name of thy Lord and Cherisher, Who created man, out of a clot of blood. Read. And thy Lord is Most Bountiful, He who taught by the pen, Taught man that Which he knew not.
>
> (Holy Qur'an 96: 1-5)

Mohammed repeated aloud what the angel had told him. He later said, 'It was as if the words were written on my heart.' The first words of the Qur'an had been revealed.

Mohammed, in great anxiety as to what all this could mean, rushed back home to his wife, Khadijah and asked her to cover him because he was shivering and to comfort him. In response to such a strange tale from her husband, Khadijah immediately told Mohammed not to worry. Allah would never disgrace him, she said, because he was such a good and honest man. For the rest of their married life together, Khadijah would be a pillar of strength, supporting her husband, Allah's Messenger. In fact, the first person to believe in the message delivered by Mohammed was Khadijah, followed by his young cousin, Ali, his close friend Abu Bakr, and Abu Bakr's servant, Zayd.

As the revelations continued, Mohammed was commanded by Allah to publicly deliver the message of Islam and to recite the verses of the Holy Qur'an which he had been given. One day, Mohammed climbed to the top of a hill named As-Safa in Makkah and began to shout for the people to come and listen to him. The people of Makkah did not know what such a commotion could mean, but since it was their trusted Mohammed who was calling them they flocked to hear what he had to say. 'If I were to warn you that an army was on the other side of this hill ready to attack you, would you believe me?' he cried out. The people said that, of course, they would believe him. 'Know, then, that I am a warner,' he said, 'and Allah has commanded me to warn you.' He warned them that unless they gave up the worship of idols and turned instead to the worship of the one Allah preached by Ibrahim they would surely perish. Some stayed to listen to what Mohammed had to say, but most turned their backs on him and walked away. His message was too much for them. They didn't want to hear.

How true and how similar this is to our own modern age. Men and women, deep down in their hearts, know what is right and yet choose to turn their backs and walk away. When a terrible tragedy afflicts mankind, such as a violent earthquake or a massive explosion causing death and destruction, people are quick to pray for help, begging the Almighty to save them. When the danger is gone, however, most of us forget our desperate dependence on Allah and we sink back to our former ways, thinking it better to run our own lives the way we choose.

The Makkahns were deeply divided over Mohammed's message, but the vast majority insulted and ridiculed him, some even saying that he had gone mad. During this time Mohammed and his followers suffered persecution at the hands of the Makkahns. The chiefs of the Quraysh became even more angry at the division Mohammed was causing and they asked his uncle, Abu Talib, to stop him from preaching his message any more. Mohammed was moved by what his uncle had to say but he said he could not ever stop calling people to Islam and the worship of Allah.

The persecution grew worse. The Muslims were ridiculed. Stones and dirt were hurled at them in the street. One hundred of them, with Mohammed's permission, left Makkah to seek refuge in the Christian land of Abyssinia. Mohammed and his followers were evicted from their homes and forced to live in a separate part of the town, cut off from everyone else. This was in the seventh year of the Revelation and it lasted for three years. No food or supplies were allowed to reach the Muslims and they went for long periods at a time with no sustenance, save the knowledge that their religion was true. Some onlookers could not bear to see such suffering continue and they secretly started to provide food to the believers. Eventually, the blockade collapsed.

Very often in life, amidst what seems a situation without hope, we suddenly find ourselves successful once more, finding help where we least expected it. This was to happen to Mohammed. In the tenth year of the Revelation, Mohammed suffered greatly. First, Abu Talib died, the uncle whom he had loved and who had protected him. Then his beloved wife, friend and companion, Khadijah, also died, leaving him alone after so many years of marriage. In this year, too, Mohammed suffered rejection from the people of Al-Taif, to whom he had gone to preach the message of worshipping one Allah alone. These people threw stones and rocks at him, causing his body to bleed.

In the midst of all this, when all seemed to be dark, Mohammed was granted an extraordinary favour. Muslims call this the Night Journey. The angel Jibril woke Mohammed from sleep and got him to mount a dazzling white steed on which Mohammed was transported from Makkah to Jerusalem, to Al-Aqsa, the furthest mosque. There Mohammed was met by an assembly of earlier prophets and he led them all in prayer to Allah. Jibril led

Mohammed from what is now called the Dome of the Rock in Jerusalem through the seven heavens, encountering prophets on the way: Adam, Jesus, John the Baptist, Idris, Moses, Aaron and, finally, the prophet Ibrahim himself. Jibril showed himself in person to Mohammed, who was dazzled by the experience, and Mohammed was taken almost to the throne of Allah Himself. It was on this extraordinary night that Mohammed was given the second pillar of Islam by Allah, the five daily prayers, which would become so fundamental to the daily life of every Muslim.

When the experience was over, Mohammed was transported back to Makkah. On his return, the disbelievers laughed even more, even calling him a liar. It was then that Mohammed and his companions prepared to leave Makkah.

Some citizens of the city of Yathrib had approached Mohammed and invited him to their city. This place was to become known as Medinat An-Nabi (Medina), the City of the Prophet. The Muslims packed up their belongings, left Makkah and their beloved Ka'aba behind and migrated to Medina. This happened to Mohammed after thirteen years of inviting people to Islam. It has become known as the Hijra, or Migration, and because of its importance in the life of Islam, the Muslim calendar now dates from this time. Just as the Christians and most of the eastern world use a calendar starting from the birth of Jesus, so Muslims have a calendar which starts from the time of the Migration. This new era was to be the second phase of the mission of Mohammed.

During this time in Medina the Muslims witnessed what was the birth of the first Islamic state, with Mohammed as its head. Islam blossomed. The centre of the state was to be the mosque. Every citizen within the state was guaranteed freedom, justice and security. Charity to all was the hallmark of this new society. Mohammed told his followers that even a smile to your brother is a form of charity. He led by example. As leader of the state he did not live in luxury, waited upon by servants, but rather lived as a simple man, sewing his own cloak, repairing his own sandals and waiting upon all who needed him. Visitors could not tell him apart from anyone else in the mosque, having to ask which one was Mohammed.

It was during this glorious time in Medina that the third and fourth pillars of Islam were granted to the believers: Zakah and Fasting. It was during this time, too, that Mohammed re-married. Another favour was granted to the Muslims. Up until this time, like the Jews, they had prayed facing Jerusalem. Now they were instructed to face Makkah whenever they prayed. So it is that today the Ka'aba is the focus of all Muslim prayer, being the first place on earth, according to Muslims, where worship was offered to the one Allah.

The Migration, then, had been a turning point in the life of the believers and in the establishment of Islam. The Muslims lived in peace and happiness in their state, ruled over by one who was as humble as he was wise. Yet they were not left completely alone. The people of Makkah looked with envy on the way they prospered and they sought to destroy this Muslim state. It was at this time that the Muslims were given permission by Allah to defend themselves from the Makkahns. In the second year of the Hijra, during the month of Ramadan, an army came from Makkah to destroy them. The Muslims were vastly outnumbered but, putting their trust in Allah alone, they managed to win the battle. This Battle of Badr was another turning point for Islam. The following year, in the Battle of Uhud, the Makkahns returned and the Muslims barely escaped with their lives, having put their trust in their weapons and strategies of war, rather than in Allah alone. In the fifth year of the Migration a Makkahn army marched on Medina and laid siege to the city for one month, but without success. They withdrew when they knew they could not succeed and the following year signed a truce with the Muslims, the Treaty of Udabiya. In all this fighting an enormous number of Makkahns and its surrounding tribes had embraced Islam, so impressed were they by the faith of the Muslims and the gentleness of their leader.

It was at this time that Mohammed wrote letters to the rulers of all the surrounding lands, including the rulers of the world's two great powers, Persia and Byzantium, inviting them to Islam. He warned that their lives and the lives of their people would be forever lost if they did not heed this call. Heraklios, the ruler of Byzantium, acknowledged the wisdom of Mohammed's message but said that circumstances were against such a change of heart. In our own age, too, circumstances often prevent us from taking decisions we know to be right. Sometimes we are just too busy to hear. Other times we choose to be deaf.

Two years after the peace treaty with the Makkahns Mohammed made an important decision. Its terms had been repeatedly broken by the Quraysh so Mohammed decided to attack Makkah. He marched on the city with an army of ten thousand and captured it with hardly any blood being spilt. In great humility, Mohammed entered Makkah on a camel with his head lowered. He granted forgiveness and amnesty to all his enemies. The third and final phase of his mission had begun. The people of Makkah voluntarily accepted Islam. The three hundred and sixty idols inside the Ka'aba were smashed into pieces and the Ka'aba was purified and dedicated once more to Allah.

Twenty-one years had passed since the first Revelation. Mohammed's life was now drawing to an end. Having seen the triumph of Islam over the idol-worshippers he returned once more to Medina, the centre of the Islamic world, and lived his life as quietly as he could, caring for anyone in need, sharing what little he owned and spending his days in praise of Allah. From Medina he sent out groups to invite all men and women of goodwill to Islam.

In the tenth year after the Hijra (A.H.) Mohammed performed Hajj, the once-in-a-lifetime pilgrimage to Makkah enjoined on all Muslims capable of making it. This was to be the fifth pillar of Islam. On the last day of the pilgrimage he delivered his Final Sermon to those present, many of whom wept as they listened. 'Remember that you will indeed meet your Lord,' he told them, so they must live in peace and charity together, without greed or usury. 'I leave behind me two things,' he said, 'the Qur'an and my example. If you follow them you will not go astray. O people, listen to my words. Know that every Muslim is a brother to every Muslim and that all Muslims constitute one brotherhood.' He called aloud, 'Be my witness, O Allah, that I have conveyed your message to my people,' and there before them he revealed the last verse of the Qur'an:

> This day have I perfected your religion for you, completed my favour on you and chosen for you Islam as your religion.
>
> (Holy Qur'an 5: 3)

At the end of the pilgrimage, Mohammed returned to his home in Medina. At the age of sixty-three he died, being buried in the earth beneath his sleeping-mat, the last Messenger of Allah to humanity.

* * *

In the city of Medina today a vast mosque replaces the simple mosque of mud bricks and palm trees that existed in Mohammed's day. A green dome stands over the spot where Mohammed's house once stood. Millions of Muslims now come to pay their respects and to pray for their Prophet, weeping in his presence.

We have said that, according to Muslims, Islam has no founder. Whilst the uneducated might venerate the tombs of holy men, seeking their blessing, Islam has no saints, as such. Mohammed was a man. At the Prophet's funeral, Abu Bakr addressed the anxious and desolate faces before him and said: 'O men, if anyone worships Mohammed, let him know that Mohammed is dead. But if anyone worships Allah, then know that Allah is alive and will never die.'

We began by saying that Moulid An-Nabi, the birthday of the Prophet, is celebrated with great joy in the district of Al-Hussein in Cairo, giving lots of fun and lots of happiness to many Muslims. Perhaps the best way for Muslims and for all people of good will to celebrate his birth, though, is to study his life and imitate his example, learning from what he said and did that he was a mercy to all mankind. May the peace and blessings of Allah be upon him.

Chapter Five

Prayer

The first thing you notice inside any mosque is just how simple it is. There isn't really much for the casual visitor to see. No elaborate side chapels, statues or paintings. Just a carpeted space for prayer. The mosque may be big or small, but the interior plan is pretty much the same - an open space with the direction of Makkah clearly pointed out on one of the walls. The Arabic word for mosque, *masjid*, quite simply means a place of prostration, so any place on earth, for the Muslim, could be his mosque. Wherever he bows down to Allah in prayer and falls prostrate on the ground before Him, that is a holy place.

The army of Amr Ibn Al-As swept into Egypt in the year 642, bringing Islam to the whole of North Africa as far as Morocco and the Atlantic Ocean. The people of Egypt, which had until that time been a predominantly Christian country, embraced Islam immediately. Cairo would become one of the major cities of the Islamic lands. Its mosques and centres of learning would be unrivalled in the Arab world. The mosque of Amr Ibn Al-As was the first mosque to be built in the whole of Africa, established so that the soldiers of Amr could pray when they first arrived in Cairo. For fourteen centuries prayer has hallowed its walls. It has been re-modelled and re-designed many times over the years, but still stands on the very spot chosen by Amr, the leader of the army of Islam. The mosque has recently been carefully and tastefully restored. It impresses now by its grand simplicity: four covered areas opening onto a large open courtyard with a covered fountain at its centre. One can only marvel at the sheer number of worshippers at Friday prayers, gathering in the mosque to pray together as a community and to listen to the weekly sermon that will feed their faith for another week.

What brought all these worshippers to the mosque was the Adhan, the Call to Prayer. Five times a day the prayer-caller announces from the minaret of every mosque that it is time for prayer, time to set aside all the cares of life in order to worship the author of Life itself. In Cairo, as in so many large cities of the Muslim world, the Call to Prayer comes first from one mosque and then, in the distance, from another and then another, until the whole city seems to be crying out to Allah, 'Allahu Akbar,' Allah is the Greatest.

Those who are not Muslim must wonder what this sound can mean. Called out in Arabic, the exact words of the Adhan are as follows:

Allah is the Greatest, Allah is the Greatest,
Allah is the Greatest, Allah is the Greatest.
I bear witness that there is no Allah but Allah.
I bear witness that there is no Allah but Allah.
I bear witness that Mohammed is the Messenger of Allah.
I bear witness that Mohammed is the Messenger of Allah.
Come to Prayer. Come to Prayer.
Come to Security. Come to Security.
Allah is the Greatest. Allah is the Greatest.
There is no Allah but Allah.

Like an air-raid siren urging the citizens to hurry and take shelter, the Adhan urges all Muslims, all of humanity, to think about Allah, to set aside all else in favour of Him, to hurry to prayer and to take shelter from the cares of life in Allah alone.

The first prayer call is followed some minutes later by a second call, announcing that the prayer is about to begin in the mosque. Muslims do not have to go to the mosque for these five daily prayers, but Mohammed taught his followers that it was better for them to do so and that they would be rewarded by Allah if they did. Every step a man takes on his way to pray in the mosque, he said, would raise him one degree in Paradise and would forgive one of his sins. It is a remarkable sight, especially on a Friday, the one day in the week when the noon prayer must be said together as a community, to see all the worshippers heading in the same direction to pray. It is a reminder to everyone that Allah is the centre of everything and that He takes priority over every other activity.

Why, then, do Muslims pray five times a day? Any Muslim would be quick to give the answer: because Allah has commanded them to do so. They believe that when Prophet Mohammed, may the peace and blessings of Allah be upon him, travelled with the angel Jibril through the seven heavens to the presence of Allah Himself, he was given the five daily prayers as the second pillar of Islam. He later narrated that at first he was told that he and his followers should pray fifty times a day. He accepted this message and began to leave, but the prophet Musa (Moses) approached him and said that fifty times would be impossible to keep. Mohammed should go back and ask that the number of prayer times be reduced. So Mohammed returned and begged that the number of prayer times be made less. Allah reduced the number to ten, so he accepted this and began to leave, but Musa again approached Mohammed. Even his own people the Jews, he said, were not capable of so much prayer. Mohammed should go back once more and ask that the number be reduced. So Mohammed returned to Allah's presence once more and begged his Lord. Allah declared that the number of daily prayers be fixed at five. Musa even thought this too many, but Mohammed felt ashamed to go back again. Allah declared, 'I have enforced My obligation and made it light for My servants. He who prays these five prayers will be rewarded as if he had prayed fifty. What I decree cannot be changed.'

We have already said that there is a deep down longing in men's hearts which craves happiness and fulfilment in life. No amount of material things can satisfy that craving. Men and women block out their thirst for happiness with as many things as they can to keep them busy. Prayer, on the other hand, answers that thirst in a real way. Prayer calms us down and puts us in touch with our real selves. Prayer is not an escape from reality. In moments of prayer we can escape to reality and see things as they really are. Prayer gives us a perspective which is true.

The five daily prayers take place at set times throughout the day: dawn, noon, mid-afternoon, sunset and evening. They give a pattern of praise and worship to daily life so that all the affairs of the day are made holy by prayer. Woken from his sleep at dawn or called from his work in the heat of the afternoon, the Muslim is summoned to forget everything else for a short while and to turn his thoughts to Allah.

Before he prays, though, he must first of all wash. There is a special routine of washing oneself that takes place before the prayer. The Muslim wants to come before the Almighty, clean. No-one would think of going to meet the President of France without having a wash. No-one would go for a job interview with dirty hands. In the same way, it would be unthinkable for a Muslim to stand before Allah without being clean. Muslims take a few moments to clean themselves before they begin. It allows the dust and the dirt of daily life to be washed away physically, just as the dust and the dirt which cling to our hearts are washed away, spiritually, by the prayer itself.

Another idea might also help us to understand the importance of the washing before the prayer begins. In some mosques built long ago, you enter via what was called a ziyada, or enclosure, which surrounded the mosque but also included a high wall to distance the mosque from its surrounding buildings. Going through the first gate from the street you would leave the hustle and bustle of life behind before walking through the enclosure to one of the doors of the mosque itself. This enclosure provided a physical break between the activity of the street and the quiet of the mosque. The washing before prayer performs a similar function. It gives the worshipper just enough time to stand apart from the world of commerce and of work and to get himself into the right frame of mind before focusing all his thoughts on Allah. Whilst he is washing he is leaving behind all that kept him busy and is declaring his intention to go and pray.

The actual prayer follows a set pattern, with different actions accompanying different words. The prayers are said in Arabic, regardless of the nationality of the one who is praying, and they involve reciting certain parts of the Holy Qur'an. When the fixed pattern of prayer has been completed, an individual may then add his own prayers, if he wants to, in any language. Those new to Islam find it difficult, at first, to master the prayers in Arabic, but the rhythm and the pattern of the prayer soon becomes natural to them. In each of the five daily prayers the worshippers recite the opening verses of the Holy Qur'an, as well as other verses they may have learned.

It is worth noting here that many Muslims take exceptional pride in knowing the whole of the Qur'an by heart, having begun to learn it as small children. Many mosques provide lessons in reading and reciting, and many schools give prizes to children who manage to recite a large number of verses on their own. It never ceases to amaze, when travelling on the metro or on a public bus in any Muslim city, how many people will be holding the Qur'an open and reciting its verses aloud, especially during the holy month of Ramadan. In many Western countries, where open displays of piety are unusual and would attract puzzled looks from onlookers, this will seem unusual. However, in the Muslim world it is wholly natural and not in the least unusual to find the person sitting next to you on a train or a bus reciting verses from the Qur'an. Such recitation is itself a form of worship. Very often, in a taxi or public vehicle, the cassette being played by the driver will not be the latest popular music but will, rather, be a cassette of this or that popular sheikh reciting verses from the Holy Qur'an.

Islam does not make any distinction between religion and life. On the contrary, for the Muslim, Islam is life itself. One of the greatest barriers to understanding Islam and the importance it has in the life of believers is this different way of looking at religion in the East and the West. In the Western world many sincere people go to their church on a Sunday and then try to put into practice during the week what they have heard on the Sabbath day. In Islam there is no Sabbath day, no day of the week holier than any other. For Muslims it is not a matter of trying their best to live a good life, based on their worship on the Sabbath. For the sincere Muslim, every moment of every day is lived in the presence of Allah. Islam is a complete way of life. Once the believer has bowed in total submission to the One Allah, all else follows on naturally. There are ways of greeting others, ways of entering a house, ways of eating which are all informed by Islam. The good Muslim will attend to his health, the way he is dressed, the way he speaks and the way he looks at other people in a way guided by Islam. He will enter the mosque in a certain way, get on a bus by greeting all those present with 'Salaamu alaykum,' and everything he sees and does will be related directly to what he believes.

No-one would think it odd or give disapproving looks to any Muslim reciting aloud the words of Allah. However, those who have not achieved the great heights of learning the whole Qur'an by heart will use what knowledge of the Qur'an they have to include different verses at different prayer times. The opening verses, though, are always the same:

In the name of Allah, the Most Gracious, Most Merciful. Praise be to Allah The Cherisher and Sustainer of the Worlds: Most Gracious, Most Merciful; Master of the Day of Judgement, Thee do we worship, And Thine aid we seek. Show us the straight way, The way of those on whom Thou has bestowed Thy Grace, Those whose [portion] Is not wrath, And who go not astray.

(Holy Qur'an 1:1-7)

The prayer is first of all praise and worship of Allah and it expresses the attitude of Muslims to Allah: they bow and prostrate themselves in humility before Him. They acknowledge that He is the Lord of everything and that nothing they do can come to any good unless it is prompted first of all by Allah. The prayer begs Allah to include the faithful worshippers in the company of those who will be saved. The rest of the prayer unfolds in the same way. The worshippers mirror what they are saying with their lips by the actions they perform, bowing or kneeling or prostrating themselves accordingly. Once again, a profound distance can be seen between this prayer of worship and praise and prevailing attitudes that have grown up in the Western world. Notions of freedom, justice and equality make many people in the West uneasy at bowing down before anyone. How unseemly, they think, for men and women to fall prostrate on the ground. And yet, for the Muslim it is wholly appropriate to bow down before Allah, to fear His judgement on the last day and to beg for His mercy. These attitudes are very real in the heart of the Muslim. We have said that the first pillar of Islam is to bear witness that there is no one worthy of worship but Allah. Muslim prayer, then, accepts that statement and puts it into practice. Muslims would find rather scandalous the idea that Allah can be talked to as an equal. Remember, Allah is without equal and has no partners, they say.

If other societies talk about freedom and equality before Allah they need look no further than the mosque. During the prayers the worshippers stand together, shoulder to shoulder, in rows, praying together without distinction of education or wealth. In the mosque you might find a prince praying next to a poor man. At the end of the prayers they will greet each other before leaving. There is no room in Muslim prayer for distinctions of class. Even the man who leads the prayers has been chosen not because he is a professionally religious person, doing a job for which he is paid, but because he knows more about Islam and the Qur'an than anyone else. There are no priests in Islam. No religious ministers acting on behalf of men. There are just Muslim brothers and sisters, bowing in submission to Allah.

Some would be quick to point out one distinction, though. They would say that the men and the women do not pray together. Surely this is a manifestation of a prejudice against women? In fact, according to Islam, the opposite is true. Islam is an eminently practical religion. The worshippers are gathered in the mosque to focus all their thoughts and attention on Allah alone. If there is a beautiful woman in the mosque it is only natural that eyes would sneak glances at her. It is neither good nor bad, but simply a fact. All of one's thoughts would be distracted. Men and women are separated in the mosque for this reason alone, to avoid perfectly natural distractions and to allow each one the privilege of prayer.

The mosque, as we have already said, is very simple. If a man prays at home he will use a small prayer mat so that the place on which he prays is clean. The area for prayer in a mosque is usually carpeted, for the same reason. There is no mystery about the prayer mat or the carpet in the mosque. Common sense says that it will keep the floor clean. The worshippers remove their shoes before entering, out of respect for the place itself and out of respect for their brothers and sisters who will be seated on the floor, lest they should bring in dust from the street. There is also in the mosque a separate place for the washing before prayer. It might be a beautifully tiled fountain or just a tap with cold water, but its function is the same.

The prayer area in the mosque will have two things: some kind of marker to point the worshippers in the direction of Makkah; and a place raised from the floor, even if only by a step or two, for the sermon to be given on a Friday.

Mosques vary greatly in size and in the way they have been built, but they all share the same basic features. Regent's Park mosque in London, for example, has a great copper dome beneath which the worshippers pray. The idea of a domed mosque developed in Islamic architecture so that the sound beneath it could be amplified and so that the hot air of the Arabian lands would rise upwards in the mosque, providing some cool for the worshippers. The dome is also a spiritual reflection of the heavens stretched above Man across the earth. The device used to point out the direction of Makkah is called the mihrab. It might be a simple curved space in the bricks of the wall or be a magnificent structure of polychrome marble and gold, but its function is simple: it amplifies the voice of the prayer leader standing in front of it and it immediately shows the direction of Makkah to anyone entering the mosque. Many mosques also have a minaret. In these days of microphones and loudspeakers it is easy for the Adhan to be broadcast. In former times, though, climbing to the top of the minaret and crying out the Call to Prayer was the best way for people to hear the Adhan above the noise and clamour of the street.

There is another small misconception, in a list of many, that some in the Western world have about Islam. Have you ever heard of the term, 'worry beads?' There are no 'worry beads' in Islam, as if they were some antidote to stress or a fanciful way to avoid smoking or biting one's fingernails. You do often see people walking in the street fingering a small set of beads, but the beads have nothing to do with worry - and everything to do with prayer. A sibha, prayer beads, consist of a string of beads that are passed between the fingers. They could be of precious stones or of simple plastic, but the individual using them will first of all say, for each bead he touches, 'Praise be to Allah.' For the second round of beads he will say, 'Thanks be to Allah,' and for the third he will say, 'Allah is the Greatest.' No hint of worry about his prayer, but a simple acknowledgement of Allah whilst the ordinary affairs of life go on. If this simple string of beads is an antidote to stress, it is not because of the beads themselves, but because of the Faith that inspires calm and peace in the heart of the believer.

So we have seen that, according to Islam, prayer is part and parcel of the life of every Muslim. From expressions of devotion that adorn everyday speech, to reciting verses from the Holy Qur'an whilst sitting on the bus, to uttering special words when entering a house or to using small beads for prayer, the Muslim's day is filled with ways of thinking about Allah. Central to all these ways are the five daily prayers given to man by Allah Himself to make holy his day. There are also quiet and private moments of prayer, either in the mosque or in the quiet of one's home. One very beautiful belief, taught to the believers by Mohammed, may the peace and blessings of Allah be upon him, is that the last third of the night, in the hours just before the dawn prayer, is a very special time for prayer. During these hours, he said, Allah descends to the lowest of the heavens, actively seeking out those who are asking of Him in prayer, so as to grant their requests. Where is the cruel and vengeful Allah that many attribute to Islam? This Allah is, rather, so tender that He stoops down to hear the prayers of His Creation. The maker of the stars and the sky, the Lord of the Worlds, stoops down.

* * *

In his poem, 'Four Quartets', T.S. Eliot very beautifully says, 'You are here to kneel where prayer has been valid.' Looking once more around the simple mosque of Amr Ibn Al-As we cannot begin to know the number of prayers which have been offered in this place. Through times of drought, plague and famine men and women have come here to ask mercy of the Almighty. In times of victory and achievement, when their daughters have been born or their sons married they have come here to give Him thanks. Praise and worship have been offered here for centuries in row after row of believers. We can only imagine the uplifted hands, the silent tears, the quiet supplications for help that have made prayer valid on this spot. 'More things are wrought by prayer than this world dreams of.' Worshippers come here from the dawn prayer to the evening prayer, many staying the whole night in between. They know that on the Day of Judgement Allah will judge them first of all on their faithfulness to prayer and on how quick they have been to respond to the prayer call. The faithfulness of some can be seen by what appears like a small bruise on the forehead, caused by one's head touching the ground so many times in prayer. The faithfulness of most, however, will be known to Allah alone, Who will reward His servants with Paradise. 'I have enforced My obligation and made it light for My servants. He who prays these five prayers will be rewarded as if he had prayed fifty. What I decree cannot be changed.'

Chapter Six

Zakah –
A debt to the poor

Attend any funeral in New York, Sydney or London and you will find one common thread linking them all. At some stage during the service the minister will speak about the one who has died. A Muslim funeral does not have this feature. When a Muslim dies, verses are read from the Holy Qur'an, funeral prayers are said and the body is buried, usually on the same day that the person died. However, at our imaginary funeral service in London the mourners have gathered to pay their last respects and they are now waiting to hear what the minister will say about the one they loved. With the coffin in full view of everyone, he will talk about the person's life. But at no funeral does the minister say how many pairs of shoes the man had. He doesn't say that he had a fast car or lots of Italian suits in his wardrobe. No-one mentions how much gold he owned or what his salary was. Instead, they talk about what kind of a husband or father he was. They might say he was a kind man or a trusted and faithful friend, hardworking and honest. Faced with death, all those things that had seemed so important in life fade into insignificance. No-one takes fancy watches with them when they die. Those who had been fooled into believing that having a lot of money made them important in this world will lie in the same kind of wooden coffin as a man who had nothing.

The third pillar of Islam, Zakah, obliges Muslims to give a certain amount of their excess wealth to those who are poor. It stands on its head the notion of acquiring more and more things at all cost and it teaches that, instead, all success and wealth in this life comes from Allah. All that the Muslim owns is owned in trust from Him. He is a steward of this life's good things. The fact that one man has a lot of money and another has not does not make either of them better or worse. All men come into the world with nothing and they leave it with nothing. Zakah, a difficult word to translate from the Arabic, does not mean charity. Muslims are not asked to give alms to the poor out of kindness. The poor have just as much right to this world's good things as anyone else and Zakah obliges those who have wealth to share a portion with those Muslim brothers who have none. This portion, then, belongs to the poor. A man has no right to keep it. It is not his and he must give it away. Zakah is a debt which Muslims pay to the poor. It is a mirror in which we see that in Islam there are no distinctions between men because of what they own. It is a mirror in which we see that all Muslims are brothers. The precise amount of a man's excess wealth which he must pay as Zakah is spelt out in detail and is rather complicated, roughly equalling two and a half per cent of what he has left over from basic necessities at the end of a year. What Zakah means is actually very simple: all men come from Allah and to Him they will return; all that they have comes from Allah and they must share a portion of what they have with those who need it.

Islam is eminently simple and eminently practical. When a man has acquired wealth which exceeds what he needs to live comfortably and to take care of his loved ones, he is asked to share the excess of his wealth with those less fortunate than he. The Communist Manifesto was to try its own form of distributing the world's wealth: from each according to his ability, to each according to his need. But in this communist world, in which there is no place for Allah, men's greed dooms such an ideal to failure. Zakah has been practiced by Muslims for centuries. Their world, created by Allah, revolves around Him, so sharing His blessings is a duty which is rewarded by yet more blessings.

That ideal world which existed when Mohammed, may Allah's peace and blessings be upon him, moved from Makkah to Medina with his companions to set up the first Muslim state, is the nearest thing the world has ever known to a Utopia. Islam was lived out in its purest form. With the mosque as its centre and the Messenger of Allah as its head, Medina was a city of charity, brotherhood and peace. Brothers cared for one another. If anyone was in need he was helped from the common treasury. So eager were the Muslims to serve Allah heart and soul that every aspect of the city's life was governed by Islam. It wasn't just a theory. It worked.

We need to understand that it was out of this lived experience in Medina that Zakah was revealed to the Muslims as the third pillar of Islam. The five daily prayers had already been revealed, and the Muslim community of Medina came together five times a day to say these prayers in common. Zakah seemed a natural progression to bind this small community even closer together.

In what was the courtyard of Prophet Mohammed's house, the believers built their mosque. Its walls were simple, of earth and baked bricks. The roof was made of date palms and the columns supporting the roof were the trunks of palm trees. Sand and pebbles covered the floor. The Prophet of Allah, may the peace and blessings of Allah be upon him, worked alongside his Companions in building the mosque. They all sang as they worked.

In this community in which Zakah was revealed there were two groups who had become Muslim: those who had emigrated from Makkah with the Prophet; and those who had already been Muslim in the city before the emigrants arrived. The newcomers were made to feel most welcome in the city. Each one was given a host family to live with and the hosts put themselves totally at their guests' disposal. Things were shared with those who didn't have enough. All were given what they lacked, since much had been left behind in Makkah, and the believers felt responsible for one another. Zakah was to be the formal obligation of what the believers were beginning to do from their hearts. In paying Zakah they would receive blessings from Allah for what they had already started to do.

There was another group, too, which existed in Medina. This was the group of polytheists (idol worshippers) and Jews who had not converted to Islam. Mohammed soon established a covenant with them, by which the Muslim and non-Muslim would live in peace and harmony, side by side. The rights of all were protected and those who were not Muslim were allowed to practice their own religion in peace. As part of the covenant agreed between Muslim and non-Muslim, all disputed matters would be referred to Allah, through His Messenger. Those who were not Muslim were not considered second class citizens in the state. After carefully establishing the rights of minorities in Medina, Mohammed began to call all to Islam, but none were coerced. The Muslim state would allow freedom of religion.

Many Muslims would ask why it isn't like this anymore. Where is the ideal Muslim state to be found, they would say. Modern attempts at this kind of Islamic state, in which all law is based on the Qur'an and the teachings of the Prophet, have met with varying degrees of success. In truth, you can't force people to be good or to be religious.

Perhaps this is why Zakah was given to Muslims. Perhaps it was given as an enduring way of protecting the weak and the poor, knowing that without this pillar to strengthen their faith, Muslims would fall prey to the greed that grows in men's hearts.

In today's world, in which we have sent manned space flights to the moon and in which one guided missile can cost millions of dollars, there are around one thousand million people trapped in abject poverty, not knowing where to find the money just to survive. In any major city in what we call the 'civilised' world, in one street you can find shoppers clad in diamonds and furs and yet in the next there are homeless young men and women begging on the street. Enough food is thrown out from shops and restaurants at the end of every day to feed an army. Mountains of food lie in alleyways eaten by rats and stray dogs.

Incidentally, Muslims are forbidden to waste food. They are conscious that many people in the world have nothing to eat. Being wasteful of food is so serious to them that they know they will be judged for it on the Last Day. That same scrap of bread which you throw away because you have had too much to eat will, on the Day of Judgement, speak out and accuse you of being wasteful. The devout Muslim is meticulous in eating everything that is placed before him on his plate. It is, in fact, considered rather impolite to say that you don't like any given food placed before you.

Prophet Mohammed, may the peace and blessings of

Allah be upon him, said that if poverty were a person he would kill him. Poverty is an evil to be wiped from the face of the earth. And yet there is no shame in being poor. Poor people, on the contrary, often have a simplicity and a generosity not to be found even in the wealthiest palace. We cannot over-generalise, but poor people often show a happiness and a thankfulness which should make their wealthier brothers and sisters feel ashamed. It is a sad fact of life that if you have everything you are often grateful for nothing, whereas if you have nothing at all, even the smallest kindness is worth so much. Poor people have a lesson to teach us all. First of all, they teach us that there, but for the grace of Allah, we too could be. Secondly, they show us that we should be thankful every day for what we have, taking nothing for granted.

If a man is poor because of what Life has dealt him, he is not to be looked upon with disdain. This disease of contempt for the poor can be found everywhere, especially among those who are so puffed up with their own importance because of what they possess. Governments from time to time have a pang of conscience and propose schemes to tackle the poverty on our streets that stares us in the face. They meet together to find ways of solving the world's poverty. Schemes to cancel the debts of the world's poorest nations, who have been tricked into debt because of the loans and the arms sales that have been lavished upon them, often result in deadlock or a failure to act. The creditor nations can't decide how much debt they can afford to cancel.

Muslims believe that Allah has given them a way to help those who are poor and weak. If properly lived, Islam redistributes the inequalities of wealth. In parliamentary elections in the United Kingdom for the last few years, one political party has suggested adding an extra one per cent on income tax and to use the extra money to spend on education. Suffice it to say that the electors did not choose this party for their government. One country recently suggested a levy on the price of all airline tickets so that the extra revenue could be used to help alleviate the scourge of HIV and AIDS. When no agreement on the proposal could be reached, it was made a voluntary levy.

The Holy Qur'an says,

> It is not righteousness that ye turn your faces to the East and to the West; but righteousness is he who believeth in Allah and the angels and the Scripture and the Prophets; and giveth his wealth, for love of Him, to kinsfolk and to orphans and the needy and the wayfarer and to those who ask, and to set slaves free; and observeth proper worship and payeth Zakah.

(Holy Qur'an 2: 177)

And it continues to say that,

> Lo! those who believe and do good works and establish worship and pay Zakah, their reward is with their Lord and there shall no fear come upon them neither shall they grieve.

(Holy Qur'an 2: 277)

So, not only is Zakah a radical way of alleviating the

suffering of those who have very little, but it also draws down blessings on those who pay it.

In the scheme of things, the number of people who have enough excess wealth in the bank to pay Zakah will never be enormous. However, Zakah is payable on excess wealth which remains in the bank for a whole year, even if that amounts only to a few dollars, so many people could be required to pay a small amount. The amount payable is two and a half per cent. There are also very complicated rules about the amount to be paid on gold and silver and agriculture and so on. It is enough that those who are not Muslim should understand the basic idea of Zakah. To understand it as two and a half per cent of excess wealth after one year is a very simple summary. Those readers who are accountants may wish to pursue the figures more closely!

And yet that simple summary, translated into real money across the globe could work marvels in the lives of millions of people. In the Muslim world the payment of Zakah does change lives. The individual Muslim may choose where the money goes, as long as he is not trying to be deceitful by paying the money to his friends or business partners. Islam gives clear guidelines as to who the recipients of Zakah might be, such as those who are genuinely poor, those in crippling debt, and so on, but the giver may choose who to give to. Many Muslims give their Zakah in secret to someone who deserves it. It is a real joy for them to see someone find money he did not previously have. Others choose to pay their Zakah directly into the poor box at the mosque, and the mosque will then distribute the money fairly amongst those who need it. Just as there is no shame in being poor, there is no shame either in asking the mosque elders for financial help.

When a terrible disaster occurs somewhere in the world we often see a generous outpouring of the goodness of the human spirit. Men and women are quick to respond to those who are in need. A drought, a famine, a terrible earthquake or Tsunami can all be the cause of great generosity and great kindness. People not only give of their money but also their time, manning phone lines or going overseas to do emergency voluntary work. Unfortunately, it is a sad fact that the media find disasters newsworthy for only a limited span of time. For a short time, drought and famine are news and they appear on news bulletins every day. However, eventually the story loses its interest and it vanishes from the headlines. People, though, do not stop starving to death in Africa just because they are no longer on our television screens. Men and women are extraordinarily generous when they are prompted to be so, but when the story moves on, life moves on, too.

A Muslim is not confined to limiting what he gives to the poor just to what he is obliged to give as Zakah. Islam places no limits on his generosity. It encourages Muslims to be kind and generous. They will be rewarded in heaven precisely by how much their good deeds have outweighed their bad. But Muslims are men and women, not angels, and they, too, sometimes need to be reminded about the poor people in their midst. Zakah is just that reminder.

* * *

Alfred Nobel is best known today for the annual prizes he established for great achievements in the world. Everyone has heard of the Nobel Peace Prize. But it took an extraordinary event to prompt Nobel's generous spirit.

Alfred Nobel introduced dynamite to the West. He was a self-made millionaire and, incidentally, not the most generous of men. It happened that the newspapers mistakenly heard that he had died and they published obituaries about his death. Nobel was naturally astonished at breakfast to read his own obituary in the newspaper. However, it wasn't just the shock of reading that he was supposed to have died that hit him so forcibly, but it was what the obituary had to say about his life. Its heading ran, 'ALFRED NOBEL, DEALER IN DEATH, DIES.' He was to be remembered by the dynamite he invented and all the suffering which it had brought to mankind, not by anything else he had done. This so disturbed and upset him that he vowed that from that moment on he would use his vast wealth for the good of mankind. He established a fund that would give prestigious awards each year to the men and women who had done most to advance mankind's knowledge of literature, mathematics and science. His most coveted award would be given to peacemakers, who had helped to resolve conflict and to bring people together.

Faced with death, not too many of us are impressed by our own wealth. It can do nothing to save us. The importance it gave us in life cannot stop our journey to the grave. When our time is up, no amount of money can stop it. The pursuit of wealth and power is what the world urges us to dedicate our lives to. Muslims believe that Islam proposes something else. All life and all its advantages come from Allah. Our lives, they believe, should be dedicated to Him. Zakah, the third pillar of Islam revealed by Allah, is a sign to men and women that there is another way. Human nature being what it is, Zakah is a formal obligation which helps Muslims to care for their brothers. It teaches them to care and it provides them with a means to do so. Out of love for Allah alone, men and women give some of their wealth to those who are poor. The poor receive this with thanks from Allah. The wealthy are blessed because of what they do. The world's natural order is turned upside down. Teaching us not to be envious of what others have, Islam, the religion of peace, establishes peace between the different members of society by sharing its wealth among them. All are led to give praise and thanks to Allah for his kindness.

Chapter Seven

Fasting During Ramadan

If you've ever been to see a film on your own in the cinema, which you really enjoyed, you will know just how difficult it is to tell your friends about the film in a way that makes it sound exciting. No amount of re-telling the story or quoting from the script can make the film come alive to your friends in the way you experienced it. You can talk about the actors, the locations and the special effects, but in no way can you make them feel your enjoyment of the film. Talking about Ramadan is a bit like this. To the casual observer, it is a month in which Muslims give up food and drink during daylight hours. It must be awful, they think, like going on an extreme diet for a month. For the Muslim, it is like a film their friends have not seen. No words can adequately convey the joy a Muslim feels in Ramadan. For them, it is like Christmas and New Year, Thanksgiving and birthdays all rolled into one. It is the holy month they have looked forward to all year round. It is a secret that only Muslims can share, and its blessings are indescribable. The fourth pillar of Islam, fasting during the month of Ramadan strengthens the Muslim believer and deepens his faith. In responding to the command of Allah, he is disciplining his body, thinking about those less fortunate than himself and renewing the principles and the practice of his own faith.

Let us turn to a different image, to make another comparison. Imagine your mother had not been to stay with you for over a year. In the Arab world this would be unthinkable, but in the West it is not beyond the realms of possibility. Imagine that the last time she came to stay she managed, just before leaving, to make a few quiet remarks about the cleanliness of your home, so that even though it was in reality very clean it managed to make you feel as though you were living in a shameful place. This time, you really make an effort to make the house look good. Floors and carpets are swept and hoovered, windows and doors washed, surfaces dusted and polished, and all the household linen washed and ironed again and again. Not just a Spring clean, but a thorough renewal of the house to prepare for your mother's arrival.

Here, the comparison ends, for Ramadan is about preparing oneself not just for the visit of a family member, dearly loved and cherished as she might be, but for standing clean and upright in the presence of Allah, Himself. In Ramadan, the Muslim tries to put his spiritual house in order, tightening up on all those things he had promised to do last year, making extra efforts to be a good Muslim. We have said that Islam means living every day in the presence of Allah, so Ramadan helps the Muslim to get back to how he would like to be. The very desire to be better, which Ramadan encourages, helps the Muslim to be better. His fasting focuses his mind throughout the day on why he is fasting. The Muslim's fast is not to lose weight or to punish himself, but is done for the sake of Allah alone. Allah has commanded the fast. The Muslim responds promptly to the command. Our comparison of cleaning the house was a trivial one. The purpose of fasting in Ramadan is far more important than pleasing another human being, however dear to us. However, if we had thoroughly cleaned our home well for our mother's arrival we would be justifiably proud of her comments when she came to stay, not finding any faults at all when she looked around. How much greater the joy of the Muslim will be, knowing that the promise of a Ramadan well kept is the forgiveness of one's sins.

Let us imagine the district of Al-Hussein in Cairo once more, although we could be describing the old heart of any Muslim city. The daylight hours of Ramadan are beginning to fade and it is approaching the time for the sunset prayer and breaking of the fast. Throats thirsting for a drink of water will soon be quenched. Men who have been toiling all day in the sun without food since dawn will soon be having their first meal. Outside every café and restaurant extra tables have been laid out to accommodate the numbers who will all be eating at the same time. In the main square, long rows of tables and chairs have been placed, 'tables of mercy,' for the poor, who will come and eat their fill without charge. Everywhere, people are waiting. Waiting for the Call to Prayer, which will signal the end of the day's fast. Radios are turned on in expectation of the prayer call. From Cairo's great citadel, built by Salah Ad-Din himself, a cannon fires to announce that the day's fast is over. Every mosque begins to proclaim, Allahu Akbar, Allah is the Greatest, and the eating and drinking begins.

Prophet Mohammed, may the peace and blessings of Allah be upon him, used to break the fast each day by first of all sipping some water or milk and then eating a few dates soaked in sugar. Many Muslims imitate him in doing this. A very strong sense of the brotherhood of all Muslims is evident. Anyone without a glass or water or a piece of bread is given something with which to break the fast. The breaking of the fast itself, breakfast, is a ritual which is a part of Ramadan. The first sip of water, the first morsel of bread, are accompanied by a prayer of thanks to Allah for food and drink. Going without food or drink all day long makes those who have been fasting acutely aware that there are many in the world whose fast will not end with the sound of a cannon or by the Call to Prayer broadcast from a mosque.

Many in the world will starve to death because they have

no food or there is no water for them to drink. For Muslims, Ramadan is a time to thank Allah for all the blessings He gives them every day – not just food and drink, but clothes, good health, work, family, friends. It helps them, too, to think of those, especially other Muslims, who need the help of others just to survive.

We need to go back now to that first night in Ramadan, Laylatul-Qadr, the Night of Power, when the angel Jibril revealed the first verses of the Qur'an to Mohammed and changed the course of human history. Muslims remember that night with great solemnity. Many spend the whole night in a mosque, reciting the Qur'an and praying for Allah's Mercy. Laylatul-Qadr reminds them that Ramadan is not only the holy month of fasting, but also the month of the holy Qur'an. Prophet Mohammed once confided to his daughter, Fatima, that Jibril visited him every Ramadan and recited the Qur'an with him.

All during the month of Ramadan special prayers take place after the evening prayer, which involve recitation of the Qur'an. By the end of the month, the whole of the Qur'an will have been recited. Muslims believe that in the last Ramadan before he died, the angel Jibril recited the whole of the Qur'an twice with Mohammed. Many Muslims make a special effort to attend these extra, Tarawiyah, prayers in the month of Ramadan. Reciting the holy Qur'an carries with it for Muslims special blessings, so many try to recite the whole of Allah's Revelation during Ramadan, to be blessed in a special way. The numbers attending evening and Tarawiyah prayers in the mosque is very impressive, being favoured over the many competing extra TV programmes during this festive season. Because Islam is at the center of the lives of Muslims, this especially religious month has a special place in their hearts. Remember, there is no distinction in Islam between religion and life. There is nothing strange about a man telling his friends he can't meet them until Tarawiyah prayers have finished, just like someone in the United States might say he couldn't meet them until after the baseball game. Islam, for a Muslim man, is a manly religion, just as for a woman it reinforces her femininity. There is no embarrassment in talking about it. Fulfilling the obligations of one's religion is considered not only natural, but admirable.

We read in the Qur'an why Muslims are commanded to fast by Allah:

> *O Ye who believe! Fasting is prescribed to you As it was prescribed to those before you, That ye may [learn] self-restraint.*

> (Holy Qur'an 2:183)

Self-restraint, then, is what Muslims are encouraged to learn. The fast begins at dawn with the first sound of the Call to Prayer. It ends with the Call to Prayer at sunset. During this time Muslims are forbidden to eat or drink or indulge in sexual activity with their spouses. Before we jump to conclusions, there is nothing wrong, in Islam, with eating, drinking or sexual activity, but abstaining from them is a form of self-restraint. It teaches one how to restrain oneself in other ways and how to work for the good of Allah alone. After the sunset prayer and all during the night until dawn the next morning, the fast is lifted and those things are lawful once more.

This fast of the Muslims in Ramadan is all-consuming. It is not a matter of giving up sweets, or putting a coin in the swear box. It is a total fast. Smoking is seen to be a form of eating and drinking, because it involves taking something into the body. Smoking during Ramadan, then, is also a part of the fast. During daylight hours the fast is a complete one and it is done for the sake of Allah. Accompanying the fast, the Muslim must also be charitable to his neighbour, since speaking or even thinking ill of others would nullify the fast.

The Qur'an goes on to say:

So every one of you Who is present (at his home) During that month Should spend it in fasting.
(Holy Qur'an 2:185)

It might be tempting to think that the best way of spending the daylight hours would be to sleep, so that the harsh effects of the fast would not be felt. On the contrary, the Muslim tries even harder during Ramadan at his work, driving himself hard to show his sincerity, not uttering a word of complaint, although he may be feeling near to exhaustion. When the Egyptian army launched a surprise attack on Israel in 1973 to regain the Sinai Peninsula it came during Ramadan. Not only that, but the attack began at two o'clock in the afternoon, when the sun was at its height and the Egyptian soldiers had been without food or drink since dawn. The attack took the Israelis completely by surprise, not least because they could never have expected the armed forces opposing them to be fasting. Such is the conviction of the Muslim about the Ramadan fast. It is total and it is done for the sake of Allah.

The Muslims were not the first ones, of course, to fast, and other religions do enjoin fasting and abstaining from meat. In the Qur'an, Allah says, 'Fasting is prescribed to you as it was prescribed to those before you.' King David is said to have fasted every week, although we do not know the precise form his fasting took. The prophet Ibrahim fasted and Mohammed, too, may the peace and blessings of Allah be upon him, used to fast even before the Revelation of the Qur'an had begun. There must be something inherent in fasting itself, then, that helps men and women to focus the mind and to do good. It teaches self-restraint. It helps the believer to live his day knowing that what he is doing is being done for Allah alone. The difference between all previous fasts and the fast of Ramadan is that, as we have said, the Muslim fast is all-consuming. It is looked forward to for a year, it is undertaken with joy and, when it is finished, it gives an immense feeling of satisfaction. The believer feels weary with well-doing. All that he has done has been done for Allah.

The Islamic calendar is a lunar one. It is based not on the movements of the sun but on the cycles of the moon. Consequently, the Islamic year, dating from the start of the Hijra (A.H.), has a certain number of days less than the Gregorian calendar used in the West, so the year is slightly shorter. This means, for example, that if one year Ramadan falls in late December, the next year it will begin in mid-December and the following year in late November, and so on. Muslims see this not just as an interesting fact, a quirk of the Islamic year, but rather a wonderful way of making Allah's blessings distributed fairly across the whole of mankind. It means that, over the years, Ramadan will take place in December or June or April or January, spreading the fast over the seasons of the different hemispheres. For example, Ramadan may one year be in the blistering August heat of Saudi Arabia, when the daylight hours stretch from very early in the morning to late at night, or another year it might be when the daylight is much less, making the number of fasting hours also less. People in Australia or Antarctica or the Sahara or Alaska will experience Ramadan in their summer or their winter, according to when it falls that year. Allah does not place an extra burden on believers because of where they happen to live. The severity or relative ease of the fast is distributed fairly across the globe. And this is only right, say Muslims. Islam is the natural religion of mankind. It knows no boundaries of time or place. Allah's Mercy is available to all who would seek it.

Experiencing Ramadan in a country which is not Muslim must be very different to a place where Muslims are all around you. In Muslim lands, restaurants and cafes will close during the hours of daylight. Who would eat in them? Schools and offices often close early, allowing those in them to get home in time for the breaking of the fast, the Iftar meal. Many businesses close completely for the month, allowing their employees holiday time when they might go on pilgrimage. Television and radio will reinforce that it is Ramadan, with many special programmes being aired. In a non-Muslim country, though, there are none of these things to support the believer. He or she must still go to work and return from it at the same time. All of his colleagues will be eating, drinking and smoking during the day. No allowance at all will be given for his fast. And yet, there are added surprises for the Muslim believer. Passing another Muslim brother or sister on the underground will give the chance for an exchanged glance, a knowing look, the knowledge of a secret shared; we are fasting for the sake of Allah. In such a situation, in such a country, the fasting of Ramadan takes on the added dimension of doing something for Allah in a land of unbelievers. It gives the Muslim a special kind of satisfaction and a special reward.

What does the fast feel like? How can people carry on their daily lives for a month without any food or drink during the day? Prophet Mohammed suggested that every night before the dawn prayer a light meal should be taken. So it is that in most Muslim households the whole family gets up in what seems like the middle of the night to sit down for a meal together. This meal, called sohoor, prepares the family members for the day ahead. There is a very lovely tradition in Cairo that dates back many centuries, which involves a man called the mesaharaty. His job is to go around the streets in the early hours banging a small drum and calling the faithful to get up to eat their sohoor before the fast begins.

Very soon after sohoor has been taken the dawn prayer will be called and the fast will begin. The fast affects people in different ways. To some it makes them feel very tired, to others it gives a headache and to others, still, it is the water that is craved for more than the food. The important thing, though, is not to let the lack of food and drink make you irritable, as that would break your fast. There would be no point to fast for the sake of Allah if you were being nasty to those around you. Consequently, Muslims behave heroically in overcoming the effects the fast produces and instead they show extra kindness to their neighbours. Prophet Mohammed suggested that in Ramadan Muslims should be even more patient and humble than at any other time. They should be very careful, he said, in what they say about others and should avoid gossip and suspicion. They should visit one another in their homes and increase the good deeds they do. Ramadan becomes a very social time, especially in the evening when the fast is over, as Muslims talk and celebrate together. As well as being a rigorous time of spiritual renewal, Ramadan is a time when the sense of Muslim brotherhood is strengthened. Those who have fasted together for the sake of Allah come together in the evening to relax and celebrate what they have achieved in the day. It gives a true feeling of satisfaction when another day's fast is successfully completed.

Everyone has heard of the word, jihad, which the television and newspapers quickly translate as 'holy war' for Islam, as though all Muslims are fanatics, waiting for the chance to blow themselves up in the presence of infidels. There are two types of jihad. The lesser jihad is to fight in the cause of Allah. There are many rules which regulate this kind of jihad, not least that it must be called for by a legitimate authority, not just any man in the street. However, there is also a greater jihad, which is much more difficult. This jihad is to live one's daily life, struggling in all things and against all odds, as a good Muslim. This greater jihad doesn't attract much media coverage. Being a good, kind and religious person doesn't make front-page news, but it is what Allah calls all Muslims to be. The ordinary days of Ramadan provide a perfect chance for the Muslim to live this greater jihad, battling against his own senses to do everything he can in Allah's name. At the beginning of every day in Ramadan the Muslim must declare his intention to fast, making it clear that he is fasting out of obedience to Allah, in response to His command and out of love for Him alone.

Can you see, now, why Ramadan is a secret which Muslims find difficult to explain, like a film they have enjoyed but can't convey to others just how much they enjoyed it? Ramadan is at the heart of a Muslim's religion. He shows in his own body what he is prepared to do for Allah, feeling the pinch of hunger and thirst and being reminded by this that he is a Muslim, called to inherit Paradise if he lives according to Allah's commands.

So the end of every day of fasting is followed by joy. Just go to that district of Al-Hussein once more. See the people enjoying the lights and the noise. They have eaten their Iftar meal as a family, have visited some friends or relatives with special sweets or Ramadan fruit drinks. They have attended Tarawiyah prayers in their local mosque and are now taking part in the fun of Ramadan nights, listening to the music and the chatter of so many happy people, happy because they have succeeded once more in fasting. The whole crowd have shared their secret; they are Muslims and they have done what Allah has commanded them to do.

Most of us, if we are truthful, will never be very famous in this world. Most of us won't appear on the television or in the newspapers. Most of us will not be called upon to do extraordinary things in our lives. We won't be the first to climb a mountain or to run faster than anyone else. We probably won't acquire vast riches or be given prestigious awards. Each person, though, is called upon to live his life as best as he can. A recruitment poster for the U.S. Marines used to say, 'Be the best you can be.' For Muslims, Islam calls all people to be the best they can be. Ramadan gives them the chance to do just that: to dedicate their days to Allah, fasting in His name, studying and reciting the Holy Qur'an, showing kindness to those around them. The world calls us to acquire more things at all costs. It tells us to become rich, and to think only of ourselves. Ramadan, on the other hand, calls upon Muslims to give up what they have for the sake of Allah, that true wealth has nothing to do with money, and to think of others less fortunate than themselves. The world rewards us with material goods. Ramadan, for the Muslim, rewards him with heaven itself.

Chapter Eight

Hajj –
The Pilgrimage to Makkah

'If I won the National Lottery it wouldn't change my life,' many are heard to say. They claim that the prospect of winning millions of pounds or dollars would not affect their daily routines. It would just make them comfortable, free of worry, they say. For others, their whole lives would be transformed. They would no longer need to work. They could have everything they wanted.

In many countries millions of people each week buy a ticket to enter a game of chance, in which one ticket will be picked out at random. The winner becomes a millionaire. Call it the Lottery or Lotto, the game is still the same: for a small price you are given a remote chance of being the winner. Leaving aside any considerations of this gambling being wasteful or even wrong, allowing us to put all our hopes in a winning set of numbers, the desire to win such a Lottery points to something more. Men and women long for something else. 'The grass is always greener on the other side,' they say. Winning the National Lottery would solve all their problems and make them happy. A lottery win, they believe, would be the chance of a lifetime, transforming dull and ordinary routines into lives of fantasy and wealth beyond imagination.

We have tried to show that Islam proposes a different set of values, where the desire for power and riches give way to a desire to please Allah and to seek His favour. By helping our brother we receive the blessing of Allah. The fifth and final pillar of Islam is what makes the heart of every Muslin miss a beat. It is what they long for and dream of all their lives. It is not winning a ticket drawn out at random. It is not a desire for millions. The fifth pillar of Islam is the once in a lifetime pilgrimage to Makkah, the Hajj, commanded by Allah, in which Muslims journey to the Ka'aba, the House of Allah, responding to His Call. The Hajj pilgrimage, for the Muslim, is better than any Lottery win. After all the struggles of life, trying to be good and trying to observe faithfully the practices of his religion, the Muslim stands before Allah in Makkah, telling Him, 'here I am. Look! I have responded to Your Call. Forgive all that I have done wrong. Look with favour on me.' With tears streaming down his face, he knows that he has come home, come home to Allah, the source of life's meaning.

The Hajj pilgrimage is enjoined once in a lifetime on every Muslim, male or female, who is capable mentally, physically and financially of performing it. In truth, many Muslims will never have the money to perform Hajj, so they will never manage to achieve it. In not doing so, they are not doing anything wrong. The fifth pillar is commanded for those who can do it. It is nonetheless the dream of every Muslim to perform the Pilgrimage, whose roots go back to the beginning of time.

The Ka'aba, or Holy House dedicated to the worship of Allah, was rebuilt by Prophet Ibrahim and his son, Ismail. The foundations on which Ibrahim rebuilt the Ka'aba go back much further in time than Ibrahim himself. One tradition says that when Adam was forgiven by Allah he built a house of worship to Allah on this spot. Another tradition says that the foundations of the Holy House were laid by angels. A third says it was built by Prophet Idris, one of the descendants of Adam. All traditions say that this place lies at the very centre of the world, and that the throne of Allah lies directly above it. Over the centuries, however, the house dedicated to Allah fell into disrepair and disuse. Men don't always keep their promises. It was the Prophet Ibrahim who was to restore it and to call all men and women to come and worship there. By the time of Mohammed, may Allah's peace and blessings be upon him, the Ka'aba had become filled with idols. It was a centre of the cult of idol worship, before Mohammed and his followers cleansed and purified it, dedicating it once more to the worship of the One Allah.

The rituals of the Hajj pilgrimage relate directly to Ibrahim, his first-born son, Ismail, and his wife Hajar, imitating what they did many centuries before.

In former times, going on Hajj was an arduous and often perilous task, as many travelled for weeks and even months to reach Makkah from distant lands. Nowadays, the pilgrims come from all parts of the globe. Packed with worshippers at any time of the year, Makkah sees an influx of around two million people every year for the Hajj, which takes place at a specific time, beginning in the twelfth month of the Islamic year. (Remember, that since the Islamic calendar is a lunar one, the time of Hajj will change each year and so can take place, over time, at any season, although its date in the Islamic calendar will always be the same.) In the past, the pilgrims would have journeyed on foot, on horses or camels. Nowadays, they fly into an international airport built by the Saudi government in the nearby city of Jeddah and are taken by bus to Makkah itself. Before reaching Makkah the pilgrims performing Hajj will bathe and put on special clothes. For the men, a white towel around the waist and another over the left shoulder. For the women, white garments covering all but the hands and face. Sandals may be worn, but not shoes. It is apparent to everyone that everyone looks the same. Everyone coming to Makkah appears equal in the eyes of Allah and of men.

Let us pause to observe what has happened. From the routines of life, millions have converged on the Ka'aba. For centuries they have left behind their families and friends, business and the cares of the world. After a lifetime of longing, they have arrived to perform the Pilgrimage. All else stops for them in this timeless moment. All around them is like a still from a film, whilst they are the ones moving. The very nature of pilgrimage means going from one place to another. What had seemed so important in life and had caused so much anxiety only a short while before, fades out of significance. The pilgrims carry with them their loved ones in their hearts, but all that weighs them down has been put aside. Every step of the pilgrimage journey is a step away from the past and a step towards a new future. By putting on ihram, the special white garments, they have cast aside the garments of the world to focus only on Allah.

Let us talk a little more about the Ka'aba itself. Pictures of the Ka'aba and its surrounding precincts, along with verses from the holy Qur'an, are to be found in Muslim homes, shops and offices throughout the world. Rebuilt over the centuries, the Ka'aba, built of stone, is square, a cube, about the size of a large house. It now stands surrounded by a vast mosque. The floor all around is tiled in white marble. The Ka'aba itself is covered with a black cloth adorned with texts from the Qur'an in pure gold. The first thing that pilgrims do as they begin the Hajj is to walk around the Ka'aba seven times. Why? Because Adam was commanded to do this, in imitation of the angels who encircle Allah's throne. The tears that flow from the eyes of the pilgrims would make a flood, as they walk around the Ka'aba for the first time, in amazement, looking upwards as it stands above them. All along the route of their journey to this place they have been calling out the Talbiyah, verses dating back to the time of Ibrahim:

'I respond to Your Call, O Allah…
I respond to Your Call and I am obedient to Your Orders…
You have no partner…
I respond to Your Call…
All the praises and the blessings are for You…
All the sovereignty is for You,
And You have no partners with You.'

Centuries before, Ibrahim had travelled from the land of Canaan with his wife, the Egyptian princess Hajar, and their baby son, Ismail. The land was desolate and inhospitable desert, but Ibrahim believed it was the will of the Almighty to come here with his small family. After some days, Ibrahim announced that Hajar and Ismail must remain behind while he returned to Canaan. Hajar was most upset to stay alone in such a place with her child, but she accepted her husband's plan, knowing that he was a good and religious man and would follow Allah's will in all things. No sooner had Ibrahim mounted his camel and left them than the baby Ismail began crying out of thirst. Seeing that there was no water to be found Hajar began to search frantically for something for the child to drink. She ran to a nearby hill called As-Safa to survey the area. Thinking she saw water in the distance near another hill called Al-Marwah she ran towards it, but to no avail, there was no water to be found. She ran in desperation, not really knowing what she was doing, seven times between the two hills, but still she found no water. To her astonishment and great relief, when she returned to Ismail she found water beginning to spring from the ground beside him. Hoping to preserve this source of water for a few days more she put a wall of sand around it, not knowing that this spring, the Well of Zamzam, would gush forth water for thousands of years to refresh the millions who would later visit this spot. Some say it was the foot of the young Ismail that had caught the ground, causing the water to spring up. Others say it was the angel Jibril himself who had struck the ground.

By the time Ibrahim returned to be with his wife and only son, other travellers had come to live in this area, finding sustenance from the spring of water which continued to flow. One day Ibrahim was told in a dream that he must sacrifice his only son, Ismail, to Allah. Not knowing why Allah should want such a thing from him, he nevertheless responded to the command of his Lord and set off at once with his young son, telling him they were going hunting. On their way to a mountain, Ibrahim and Ismail were approached by a man who urged Ibrahim not to carry out Allah's will. Ibrahim threw seven stones at this stranger, who he knew to be Satan in disguise, and the man left. Satan reappeared in a different guise and this time Ismail threw seven stones at him to make him go. For a third time, Satan came and whispered to Ibrahim not to carry out his mission. Ibrahim threw another seven stones and Satan disappeared. He then explained to his son what was to happen. The young Ismail replied:

O my father! Do As thou art commanded: Thou wilt find me, If Allah so wills, one Of the steadfast.

(Holy Qur'an 37:102)

With grief in his heart, Ibrahim raised a knife to kill his son as a sacrifice to Allah. The knife pressed against the boy's flesh but would not cut. He suddenly heard a voice calling out,

You have fulfilled the dream.

(Holy Qur'an 37:105)

and a ram came down the mountain just at that moment. Ibrahim and Ismail, with joy in their hearts, offered the ram, instead, as a sacrifice to Allah.

Ibrahim is known to Muslims as the Intimate Friend of Allah. His life was one of total obedience to the Almighty. He was to have a second son, Isaac, with his other wife, Sarah, who lived in Canaan, and he would travel between the two families. When Ismail had grown to manhood, Ibrahim heard the Call to build a house in honour of Allah. Father and son built on a red mound of earth, revealed to Hajar in a dream, finding beneath it some already existing foundations. They together rebuilt the Ka'aba, the first house on earth built in honour of the One Allah. When the Ka'aba was complete Ibrahim was commanded:

And proclaim the Pilgrimage Among men: they will come To thee on foot and [mounted] On every camel,

*Lean (on account of journeys) Through deep and distant
Mountain highways.*

(Holy Qur'an 22:27)

This place was still desert, with very few inhabitants, but Ibrahim obeyed at once, calling out to the wilderness in the north, south, east and west that men and women should come to worship at this place. From the distance in all four directions he heard the extraordinary words coming back to him, 'I respond to Your Call, O Allah…. I respond to Your Call,' and vast throngs appeared from every direction to worship at the Ka'aba. Ibrahim, the Intimate Friend of Allah, asked for the rituals of the pilgrimage to be revealed to him and they were explained to him by Jibril.

And so it is today that those performing Hajj carry out a precise ritual, rooted in the obedience of Ibrahim and his family. Ibrahim was asked to leave his own country and set forth into a barren and wild place, putting his trust in Allah alone. He was asked to sacrifice his only son, the dearest thing in his life, in obedience to Allah. Hajar was obedient to Allah and prompt to listen to her husband. Her search for water for her baby resulted in finding the well of Zamzam. Ismail was so devoted a son and so responsive to the Call of Allah that he was prepared to die if it was a part of Allah's unknown plan.

All of these thoughts are in the mind of the pilgrim as he or she moves slowly from one place to another during the Hajj. The pilgrim, too, has been called to leave his country and put his trust in Allah alone. He is asked to give up everything that is dear to him, if Allah so wills, and to respond promptly to His Call. The Hajj pilgrimage comes as the summit of a Muslim's life. He is prepared to give his very life, if it should be required to give glory to Allah.

Most pilgrims coming from overseas arrive at King Abdulaziz International Airport in Jeddah. From there they usually travel by bus to Makkah. Before entering the city their documents are checked. Each one must prove that he is Muslim. So holy is Makkah that non-Muslims are not allowed to enter the city. All during the bus journey the pilgrims have been chanting together, in Arabic, 'I respond to Your Call, O Allah... I respond to Your Call....' Excitement mounts as they approach. Over the next days they will re-enact a timeless tradition. Seven times they will circumambulate the Ka'aba, as Adam was commanded. Seven times they will run between the hills of As-Safa and Al-Marwah, in imitation of Hajar's desperate search for water. They will throw stones at a pillar representing Satan, symbolically casting away all those things in their lives which prevent them from doing Allah's will.

All of these rituals culminate in an extraordinary moment in time, which mirrors the Day of Judgement itself. We said right at the start that before the creation of Adam, Allah gathered the souls of everyone who would ever exist and told them on the plain of Arafat, a valley just outside Makkah, that He is Allah and that there is no other. It was to Arafat that Adam came seeking and receiving Allah's Forgiveness and Mercy. Muslims believe that on the Day of Judgement all souls will once more assemble on the plain of Arafat and give an account to

Allah for their deeds. They will receive a written record of all that they have done and will answer for their actions in front of everyone else. Nothing will remain hidden. Their sins and their good deeds in this life will be made known to everyone. And they will be judged for them.

In what most people see as the culmination of the Hajj, the pilgrims stand for hours on end in the blazing heat on the plain of Arafat: up to two million people, dressed only in white cloths, begging and pleading with Allah. The joy of seeing the Ka'aba for the first time is now in stark contrast to the deep sadness the pilgrims feel for their sins. It is as though their whole lives appear before them and in this once in a lifetime pilgrimage they are making amends for what they have done and are seeing what could have been. It is little wonder that the pilgrims are crying. Not many of us get a chance in life to review how we have lived and resolve to change and be better. The Hajj pilgrimage provides just that chance. It never ceases to amaze how men and women of over eighty years of age find the strength to stand for so long in the midday sun at Arafat. Yet they do. No-one would think of sitting. The stand at Arafat is the turning point in the pilgrimage. It is the turning point in the pilgrim's whole life. There is no going back. They have made the Pilgrimage. They have stood in honesty before Allah, admitting who they are and what they have done.

We are very clever at presenting masks to those around us. Sometimes we wear the mask of the victim. At other times we wear the happy mask, even though we might be crying deep inside. All that people are allowed to see of us is what we show them. We have become very clever at it. We can fool almost everyone. Some of us are so clever at wearing these masks that we can even fool ourselves. But Allah is not to be fooled:

> *Truly, nothing is hidden from Allah, in the earth or in the heavens.*

(Holy Qur'an 3:5)

At Arafat the pilgrims take off the mask, standing symbolically naked before Allah, just as on Judgement Day they will stand physically naked before Him on this spot. Their response is to weep: tears of sadness for all the missed opportunities and for all the things they have willfuly done wrong; and tears of joy for the Mercy and Forgiveness they receive from the All-Merciful One. They have performed the pilgrimage.

However, there is one further ritual to be performed before the Hajj is complete. Like so many of the Hajj rituals this is done in remembrance of what Ibrahim did, offering to sacrifice his only son and being told, instead, to sacrifice a ram. The pilgrims sacrifice a sheep in imitation of Ibrahim's sacrifice. Some of the meat is taken by the pilgrims themselves, whilst the rest is given to the poor. How though, we might ask, does the blood of a sheep, or its meat, give honour to Allah? Clearly, in itself it does not and it adds nothing to His glory. Allah made the sheep. We are not giving Him anything He does not already have. Allah is not pleased by the blood or the meat of the sheep, but by the obedience and thankfulness of His servants.

This part of the Hajj pilgrimage is celebrated as a feast throughout the Muslim world, the feast of Eid Al-Adha. Millions of Muslims have followed from afar the rituals of Hajj and they now celebrate the feast together.

As with the other Muslim feast, which comes at the end of Ramadan, Eid Al-Adha is a time when children are bought new clothes and given money by their relatives. The pride with which a little girl shows off her new dress to the world is just another sign of the joy that Islam brings. The family comes together for a meal and to celebrate.

By way of a brief pause, we cannot allow to pass unnoticed the gaping difference between the way Muslims celebrate their two feasts and the way Christmas has come to be celebrated in many parts of the world. Unfortunately forgetting the real reason and the true spirit of Christmas, media and marketing experts have turned it into a shopping extravaganza. From August onwards the shops entice us with promises of bigger and better presents, fuelling the greed of those who want more and more. We intend here no slight on the feast itself, as many do celebrate with great sincerity the birth of the one they believe to be their saviour, but Christmas has been stolen from them by the advertising companies. No such hype, however, accompanies the two Muslim feasts. A few days off work, a celebratory meal and time with the family are the essence of the feast, after the special community prayers have been said. The Muslim feasts are precisely that: religious celebrations.

In conclusion, then, to mark the end of the Hajj pilgrimage, the pilgrim's head is shaved and he goes to make a final circumambulation of the Ka'aba. His heart is full of joy and sadness at the same time. Joyful because he has achieved his life's dream. Sad because he knows he will probably never come here and see this place again. After his last gaze upon the Ka'aba, fixing its view upon his heart, the pilgrim begins to return home, taking with him blessed memories and the countless blessings he has received. In many parts of the Muslim world, those who have performed the pilgrimage will paint on the outside of their homes a picture of the Ka'aba and the method of transport they used to get there. In the Arab world, those having made the Pilgrimage will from that time be addressed as 'Hajj,' and looked up to with respect as one set apart from men, one who has achieved the goal, gained the prize and fulfilled the ambition of a lifetime.

Most Muslims will never reach Makkah. Even after a life of continuous toil, most will not be able to afford to go on the Pilgrimage. Those who have been, then, are even more like the winners of the Lottery. The prize they have won, though, is not just the passing allure of money or a fast car or a holiday in Spain. The fifth pillar of Islam, going to Makkah on Pilgrimage in obedience to Allah, is what the Muslim's heart has desired all his life. After the Pilgrimage the heart can rest. Obedience to Allah is its own reward.

Chapter Nine

Gardens of Delight

And so, what of the Gardens of Delight promised in the book's title? Where are they to be found? The answer is simple: in Paradise. The Muslim has looked forward to them all his life. But before we reach them we need to digress and step back once more into the busy streets of Cairo.

* * *

Darb Al-Ahmar, a sprawling street of centuries old workshops, mosques and once grand Ottoman houses, lies just outside the southern gate of the city, Bab Zuweyla.

The city walls themselves have been so encroached upon by the surrounding buildings that you only notice them when they are almost upon you. In the Middle Ages Cairo had burst its existing walls because the growing population could no longer be contained within them. Merchants and princes had now to build their houses and palaces outside the walls of the city. They chose this street, Darb Al-Ahmar (the Red Street), as it led to Cairo's Citadel, the massive fortress built by Salah Ad-Din to maintain his hold on the city and to protect it from any threat from Crusader armies. Sitting in a café nowadays, sipping mint tea and watching the world go by, we can almost see the Sultan's ministers coming out of the city gate in search of the first sighting of the new moon, which would herald the start of Ramadan. We might even see the Sultan himself, preceded by a grand procession, riding along this street at the start of the annual pilgrimage to Makkah. If he could not go in person, we would see covered copies of the holy Qur'an travelling in state instead of him. Along this street building space was at a premium and many architects and builders were ingenious in the way they managed to conceive a mosque entered from the street and yet still managing to maintain that it faced Makkah. It is to one such a mosque that our digression has led us. The mosque of Al-Maridani. Built in 1339, it gives no hint from the street as to what lies inside.

The whispers and the hushed, reverent tones that prevail in many a Baroque church are not to be found in a mosque. Ladies in gloves and feathered hats have no place here. It is because a mosque is not only a place for prayer. It is also a place of learning, a meeting place and a place of rest. It is not unusual to see a group of friends chatting quietly, another group sitting listening to a teacher speaking to them about the Qur'an, and a third group simply asleep on the floor. This last activity seems strange and somehow irreverent to those used to churches. It is not encouraged to lie on the floor and go to sleep in a church! However, the mosque is a place of rest from the heat of the day.

Al-Maridani mosque provides cool and rest from the busy street. The activity, the dust and the bustle of life on Darb Al-Ahmar are in stark contrast to the quiet within. Somehow, the mosque mirrors the difference between the harsh reality of life in this world and the rest promised to us in the world to come. From the dust of the road we enter a garden. Trees and shrubs provide shade and shelter from the sun. The trickle of water can be heard, refreshing the spirit before it is used to cleanse the body. It is such a surprise from life on the street. Around this garden are those intricate wooden lattice-work screens known as mashrabeya, which cut out the direct sunlight from the prayer area. The small windows, high up in the walls, have been made into colourful patterns with small pieces of glass, to filter the light and maintain a calm, cool, shaded atmosphere. The smell of the trees gives a welcome break from the harsh smells of the street. It is here in this garden that many Muslims have come over the centuries to make their prayers in the mosque and to take a break from their work to contemplate the beauty of Nature. Flowers, shade, shrubs, water all remind them of something else. Coolness and calm remind them of another garden, a garden with rivers flowing underneath in which their every desire will be fulfilled; the garden which is Paradise.

* * *

Whilst the Qur'an is universal and knows no boundaries of place or time, it was revealed to Mohammed, may the peace and blessings of Allah be upon him, in the harsh desert of Arabia to a people used to thirst and to blistering heat. How beautiful for them, then, to hear a description of what life will be like for them in heaven:

> But those who believe And do deeds of righteousness, We shall soon admit to gardens, With rivers flowing underneath... We shall admit them to shades, cool and ever deepening.
>
> (Holy Qur'an 4: 57)

We have already said that it is impossible for the human mind to conceive what Allah is like. The more we think we understand what He is like we can be sure that He is not like that. Allah is beyond our understanding. In a similar way, we cannot really conceive of heaven. Heaven is so different from earth that our language fails us. Muslims are given an image of heaven in the holy Qur'an which is really beautiful. They have no other image than the one Allah has given them.

Just before his death, Prophet Mohammed, may the peace and blessings of Allah be upon him, stretched out his hand as if reaching for something. 'I saw Paradise,' he said, 'and I reached out for a cluster of its grapes. Had I taken it, ye would have eaten of it as long as the world endureth.' The image of Paradise, for Muslims, is truly delightful and it corresponds directly to what hearts longing for refreshment and bodies weary for rest are searching for. The Garden is what all hearts have desired. It is truly a Garden of Delights.

In this Garden no-one will ever be weary. Each one can eat and drink without ever feeling full. All will recline on couches. No-one will ever feel pain or want for anything. In this Garden of Paradise the inhabitants will all be dressed in garments of green silk and will wear bracelets of gold and fine pearls. The heat will never touch them and they will never tire:

> Therein are rivers of water unpolluted, and rivers of milk whereof the flavour changeth not, and rivers of wine delicious to the drinkers, and rivers of clear-run honey; therein for them is every kind of fruit, with pardon from their Lord.
>
> (Holy Qur'an 47: 15)

It is important to remember how Muslims look upon life in this world for us to understand fully their belief about life in the next. Just try to imagine a boy sitting at the roadside in Darb Al-Ahmar waiting to shine shoes. He has had little breakfast and the sun is hot, but he has a smile on his face and a cheery greeting for those who pass by. When asked how he is, he will reply, 'Alhamdulillah,' thanks be to Allah. Heaven and Hell are as real to him as the nose on his face. Heaven is not imaginary pie in the sky. It is real. Hell is not a caricature of all that is bad. It is, for him, a real place where people will be punished for all eternity. The Day of Judgement is real. On that day all men and women will be rewarded with heaven for the good they have done or cast into hell on account of their bad deeds. Our boy has said his prayers and he is kind and generous with what little he has. Why should he be envious of that man with a big car? The man's car won't save him if his deeds are bad or if he neglects his prayers. Our time on earth is short. Allah tests us to see how we will respond to His will.

This boy has been taught from an early age that he is on the earth for a definite purpose and for a fixed time. Allah knows everything he will ever do and there is nothing that will ever happen to him that is not a part of Allah's plan. He has nothing to fear, for Allah is protecting him and He will never place a burden upon him that he cannot bear. If he does experience hardship or suffering in this life he must bear it with patience because suffering, too, is a part of Allah's mysterious plan. The trials and tribulations of life, when accepted with faith in Allah, will draw down their own blessings. No matter how poor he is in this life he has a glorious future waiting for him, if Allah wills, in the world to come.

Gardens of Eden! They enter them wearing armlets Of gold and pearl. And their raiment therein is silk. And they say: Praise be to Allah Who hath put grief away from us. Lo ! Our Lord is Forgiving, Bountiful. Who, of His Grace, hath installed us In the mansion of eternity, Where toil toucheth us not Nor can weariness affect us.

(Holy Qur'an 35: 33-35)

In a similar way, the boy knows that just as his efforts to be good will be rewarded, all of those in this world who do evil will be punished. It may seem that sinners' ways do prosper here on earth, but sinners will get their comeuppance. Those laughing now in lives of wickedness will weep for ever in the fires of hell.

Just as the description of heaven is beautiful, the description of hell in the Qur'an is graphically horrific. Even in the grave a man will begin to experience the punishment he is due. The walls of the grave will squeeze in on him, crushing his body. Worms and insects will bite him in the grave, and angels will prod and beat him with iron rods. Through a window he will see the horrors that await him: the burning fire and the smoke; the boiling water which will be given him to drink; the total despair. At any time in his life a man might repent and turn his back on his sins, turning instead to Allah, who will be waiting for him with Mercy and Forgiveness. Once a man dies, however, there is no repentance. He cannot make up for what he has done. All Muslims know that they could die at any moment and they pray that they will die with the words of the Shahadah on their lips: I bear witness that there is no Allah but Allah. And I bear witness That Mohammed is the Messenger of Allah.

Our boy sitting by the side of the road in Darb Al-Ahmar knows that the Day of Judgement will be a day of justice. All those who have had their rights taken away from them will have them restored. Those who have been victims will have a right to justice from their oppressors. Even those who were cruel to animals will be repaid for their cruelty by the animals themselves.

And yet, Allah, the Merciful and the Compassionate One, will also show tenderness and mercy. There is a tradition, attributed to Mohammed, may the peace and blessings of Allah be upon him, which speaks of the tender mercy of Allah. When all people are handed the written record of their deeds on the Day of Judgement, he said, one man will listen carefully to his record. When it is finished and all his bad deeds have been read out loud he will put up his hand and say, in front of Allah, that something has been missed out, that he did something else very bad, but that it has been forgotten. Allah will tell him, 'Hush, no need to mention that. I know the secrets of your heart. Let it be forgotten.' Similarly, another man will listen to his good deeds being read out and, when he has heard them all, he hears one more good deed that he did not do, that he built a mosque for the sake of Allah. He will put up his hand and say, in front of Allah, that a mistake has been made, he did not build a mosque. Allah will reply to the man that for the many times he prayed during his life on earth, with tears in his eyes, vowing that if he had the money he would build a mosque for the sake of Allah, it would be written in the Book as if he had actually done it. Allah is Merciful and Compassionate.

The righteous will be led into Paradise and the evil-doers into the hell fire.

> Thou seest the wrong-doers Fearful of that which they have earned, And it will surely befall them; While those who believe and do good works [will be] in flowering meadows of the Gardens, having that which they wish from their Lord. This is the great preferment.
>
> (Holy Qur'an 42: 22)

As he goes into the mosque to take a few moments of rest from the day's work, to wash himself and then to pray, our young boy know that he is destined for glory, if he can cling to what is right and do good. The Five Pillars of Islam hold up his faith, offering him a glorious reward for a life well-lived.

> Reclining therein upon couches, they will find there neither [heat of] a sun nor bitter cold. The shade thereof is close upon them And the clustered fruits thereon bow down. Goblets of silver are brought round for them, and beakers [as] of glass... Their raiment will be Fine green silk and gold embroidery. Bracelets of silver they will wear. Their Lord will slake their thirst with a pure drink.
>
> (Holy Qur'an 76: 13-15,21)

And so our young boy - we might call him Ali or Hassan or Mohammed - finishes his prayers and goes back out into the street. He leaves behind the cool and the shade of the

115

mosque, with its garden of shrubs, flowers and palm trees, and returns to his spot by the side of the road. He will hope to earn enough money cleaning shoes not only to buy himself something to eat later in the day, but also to take money back home to his mother. He is young, but he is the man of the house and what he takes home will help to feed his brothers and sisters. Even though our boy has nothing to boast about in terms of honours or wealth, he is still smiling. The heat of the day and the dust of the street have not diminished his capacity to smile one little bit. And why? Because like so many millions of his brother Muslims, he is part of the secret. It is as though he, too, has been to see that film that he can't fully describe in words. Our boy is Muslim and that makes him happy. He is so proud of it that, with a smile, he will ask foreign tourists what religion they are when they stop to make conversation with him.

Non-Muslims are usually taken by surprise when their Muslim neighbours ask them what religion they are. In the Western world people have become accustomed to steering clear of religion as a topic of conversation. Remember, they are brought up not to talk about religion or politics at the dinner table. This avoidance of religion is then extended to the newspapers and the television screen, so that eventually religion becomes a taboo subject. The only ones talking about religion are, on the one hand, extremists and fanatics and, on the other, people who are decidedly weird. Various surveys in recent years have claimed to show the decline in belief in Allah among people in the United Kingdom.

Whether this is true or not, there has certainly been a decline in adherence to organised religions or religious practice. This is apparent at any religious service. The numbers are going down.

Something happened, though, a few years back to show how people are still concerned about spiritual values. Diana, Princess of Wales, was killed in a car crash in Paris. The whole world was stunned as they heard the news. It is not an exaggeration to say that the British people were traumatised by the event. For a whole week the nation witnessed something extraordinary. Thousands of people descended on London to leave flowers outside Buckingham Palace, the home of the British Queen, and Kensington Palace, the Princess' home. By the end of the week the aroma of flowers was overwhelmingly lovely. For a whole week newsreaders on television wore black ties and sat at news desks backed by purple or black drapes. London had not seen anything like this for years. On the day of the funeral itself, thousands lined the route of the funeral procession or waited in public parks to watch the funeral on giant television screens. Westminster Abbey, for centuries the scene of countless coronations, royal weddings and state funerals, erupted into popular applause for the Princess. A pop singer was chosen to sing about Diana, the People's Princess. Hysterical crowds followed the funeral cortege as the coffin was taken to its final resting place.

Why this digression to Princess Diana? What has it to do with Islam? Well, what happened during that extraordinary week at the end of an English summer in 1997 pointed to something much more significant than the death of a princess. The British people were stricken with grief. Businessmen, visibly moved, left their offices at lunchtime to lay a single rose in the princess' memory. Millions were glued to their television screens. It is not too far-fetched to suggest that people were actually mourning the death of goodness itself. What we witnessed was a yearning for values which lay long hidden, deep within the human soul. People burst out crying for no reason, because a religious chord in their hearts had been touched, which had been left dormant for years. In a world in which religion had been dismissed as irrelevant or eccentric, people were suddenly confronted with spiritual questions: Why are we here on earth? Why do the good die young? What kind of Allah allows the good to suffer? Is there a Allah at all?

There might well have been a decline in religious practice or of belief in organised religions in the West, but Islam tells us that the human heart is made for Allah. What all those people were experiencing was their innermost self crying out for something denied them for so long. Remember, all roads lead to Allah.

Our young boy knows the answer to all those questions about life's meaning. Islam has taught him. There is no distinction for him between religion and life. He is neither weird nor an extremist nor a fanatic. He is just a perfectly ordinary young man trying to earn enough money to feed himself and his family. Does praying make him a fanatic?, he asks. Does trying to help others less fortunate than him make him weird? Does dreaming about going on a once in a lifetime pilgrimage to Makkah make him an extremist? We often fear that which we don't understand. Islam is much misunderstood in today's world. If our only knowledge of Islam comes from distorted news headlines we are sure to live forever in fear of what we don't really know. If we can begin to see Islam through the eyes of Muslims themselves, like our young shoeshine boy, we might begin to understand.

Muslims remain bewildered that their religion is not only misunderstood but vilified as a religion of fanatics. Our young boy, Ali or Hassan or Mohammed, knows that Islam is the religion of peace. Misunderstood by many who are not Muslim, he will carry on through the harsh realities of life trying his best to be a good person. Several times a day he will declare his belief in the oneness of Allah and that Mohammed is His Messenger. He will go quickly to pray when he hears Allahu Akbar from the mosque. He will pay Zakah if ever he has enough money to pay it, but he will always think of those even less better off than he. He will look forward all year to the coming of Ramadan, when he will fast with all his heart and soul during daylight hours. And it will be his life's dream to go on pilgrimage to Makkah, in response to Allah's call.

His hope and his prayer will be that when his time on earth is over, he will look back on a life well-lived. He has lived the secret, according to the principles of Islam. Now he will hope to hear these words of the Qur'an, as if Allah were addressing them to him alone.

> But ah! thou soul at peace! Return unto thy Lord, Content in His good pleasure! Enter thou among my servants! Enter thou my Garden!
>
> (Holy Qur'an 89: 27-30)

Related titles published by Stacey International:

The Concise Encyclopædia of Islam, by Cyril Glassé
Hardback, ISBN: 978-190098-80-63, £45.00
Paperback, ISBN: 978-190098-85-44, £24.95

What is Islam? by W Montgomery Watt
Hardback, ISBN: 978-190098-86-74, £25.00

The Origins and Early Development of Shi'a Islam,
by S H M Jafri
Hardback, ISBN: 978-190529-93-62, £25.00

Order online at:
www.stacey-international.co.uk